IN SPEECH AND IN SILENCE

ALSO BY DAVID J. WOLPE

The Healer of Shattered Hearts:
A Jewish View of God

David J. Wolpe

IN
SPEECH
AND
IN SILENCE

The Jewish Quest
for God

HENRY HOLT AND COMPANY
NEW YORK

Published by Henry Holt and Company, Inc.,
115 West 18th Street, New York, New York 10011.
Published in Canada by Fitzhenry & Whiteside Limited,
91 Granton Drive, Richmond Hill, Ontario L4B 2N5.

Library of Congress Cataloging-in-Publication Data
Wolpe, David J.
In speech and in silence : the Jewish quest for God /
David J. Wolpe.—1st ed.
p. cm.
Includes index.
1. Language and languages—Religious aspects—Judaism—Meditations.
2. Silence—Religious aspects—Judaism—Meditations.
3. Judaism—20th century—Meditations.   4. Spiritual life—Judaism—
Meditations.   I. Title.
BM538.L34W65 1992
296'.014—dc20   92-11539
                                                                      CIP
ISBN 0-8050-1678-3 (acid free)

Henry Holt books are available at special discounts
for bulk purchases for sales promotions, premiums,
fund-raising, or educational use. Special editions
or book excerpts can also be created to specification.
For details contact: Special Sales Director,
Henry Holt and Company, Inc., 115 West 18th Street,
New York, New York 10011.

First Edition—1992

Designed by Kate Nichols
Printed in the United States of America
Recognizing the importance of preserving the written word,
Henry Holt and Company, Inc., by policy, prints all of its
first editions on acid-free paper. ∞

1   3   5   7   9   10   8   6   4   2

*Translations of biblical material are from the Jewish Publication Society Bible,
TANAKH (1985), except where a difference of emphasis or nuance necessitated
another translation. Translations of rabbinic materials are the author's own.*

To my Mother,
with the prayer that some of these words
might speak for her

Contents

Acknowledgments

I feel very fortunate to be able to write and teach at the University of Judaism. Over the years, Dr. David Lieber, now President Emeritus, has managed to forge a truly unique institution. I am grateful to him personally, and to the wonderful school he did so much to create.

My adult interest in the study of Judaism was the product of an encounter many years ago with Dr. Elliot Dorff, who is the rarest of all academics: a philosopher whose goodness matches his learning. My first steps in Jewish philosophy were taken with Elliot's deft guidance, and his counsel and aid have been indispensable ever since. Were it not for Elliot's influence I, like countless other Rabbis and teachers of Judaica, would never have entered this marvelous world.

This book owes a great deal to the President of the University of Judaism, my colleague and friend Rabbi Robert

Wexler. The Mishna counsels that one wishing to learn should "find oneself a teacher, and make oneself a friend." Rarely are those two roles filled by the same person. Bob was one of my first teachers, and he has become my friend. His insight and encouragement made this book better. It is no exaggeration to say that his friendship made it possible.

Marian Wood once again provided the combination of intuition and editorial expertise that every author hopes to find in an editor. As both critic and champion, Marian is unexcelled.

A number of friends and colleagues contributed to this work, which would be poorer without their help: I would like to thank Sam Mitnick, Nama Frenkel, Mimi Sells, Marc Platt, and my teacher Dr. Elieser Slomovic, all of whom gave generously of their time and expertise.

My brothers, Steve, Paul, and Danny, and my sister-in-law Valerie understand and share on the deepest level the incidents and themes this book discusses. I am grateful to them for their ideas and for their love.

As with everything I write, what follows is saturated with my father's teachings. Not only did he carefully and repeatedly review the manuscript with me but he has always been, in his words and in his life, in his gentleness and in his wisdom, an embodiment of the ideals this book seeks to explore.

Finally, *In Speech and In Silence* is a tribute to my mother. Her illness initiated these explorations. Her continuing trials inform each page. But this book did not come from a sense of defeat. It came from an appreciation of her vivid character, her sharp judgments, her valor. My mother's strength and struggle invite not a lament, but a celebration.

Preface

Words can reach to the depths of our nature. They echo inside when we are moved, angered, despairing, or joyous. In moments of great feeling, we search for the right words, though they elude us. Somehow experience is not full until we can frame it in language. Love unspoken is incomplete.

Our life is bracketed by the wonder of words: we celebrate the first prattle of infancy, strain for the concluding wisdom uttered in last moments. Words are the currency in which we trade the information, the sentiment, the stuff of human life.

Words can capture us, and often outlast us. "The world will little note, nor long remember, what we say here," said Lincoln in his address at Gettysburg, "but it can never forget what they did here." Yet more than a century later, when the names of the soldiers who died are mostly forgotten, Lincoln's words are indeed what is remembered about Gettysburg, and the heroism itself is recalled largely because Lincoln poured his eloquence upon the field of battle.

Studying old works of religious importance, I am constantly astonished by the vitality of words inscribed by a stylus on paper or parchment generations ago. Long after the authors of sacred texts are forgotten, the words they have crafted change lives; ancient words continue to instruct, to infuriate, to inspire. Words are the vessels in which the past is carried into the present.

They are also the vessels in which human connection is carried. The ability to speak what is inside us is a central force in human relationships. Daily conversation—the telling of anecdotes and incidents—offers others familiarity with the patterns of our lives. There are also truths about ourselves that we reserve for the few, the deep-speaking saved for those who are special to us. The bonds are more intimate than we can say, but the need to express them is an inescapable part of the connection: I can never tell you all that is inside me, but in the attempt we draw close.

People are partial to their own work, their own world. The way we spend our lives, the activity that absorbs us, comes to seem singularly valuable. Architects look with a special eye and appreciation at the cornice, the copestone, and the beveled plane. To a designer, fashion is not an addition to the human form, but of its essence. To anyone who works with words, they sum up human experience.

As someone who writes, and who is engaged in a tradition so devoted to words, I have always felt words to be particularly precious, the magic current carrying much of the electricity of life. Judaism instructs us in the vitality of words. Through study and discourse, in sacred texts and prayer, what can be expressed assumes an enormous importance. Ultimately Judaism judges life by action, by deed; it is a system that stresses the importance of proper conduct. Yet it never relinquishes a sense that language can reach to the center of our souls.

In what follows we will trace words in their enchanted path through our lives and through one particular tradition. All the while we will be seeking to uncover not only what words can say, but what they cannot say. The path will take us through legend, through biography, through personal tragedy. With each new understanding of speech, with each exploration of song, with each deepening appreciation of prayer, we will be straining toward silence. For speech and silence together form the path that leads to the presence of God.

We pray that God may accept

our call for help. But we also pray

that God, who knows that which is hidden,

may hear the silent cries

of our souls.

RABBI URI OF STRELISK

ONE

~

The Spirit of Speech

The final moments of Rabbi Ishmael:
During the second century of the common era
those who remained faithful to Judaism were
persecuted and killed by the Romans. Sages and
scholars who had continued to teach Torah in
defiance of imperial decrees met their death as
retribution for their devotion.

Rabbi Ishmael was captured by the Romans and
sentenced to death. He endured the tortures inflicted
upon him in silence. Finally, unable to contain his
suffering any longer, a cry escaped his lips. Taking
note of the anguish of this pious man, God
declared: "If one more word comes from Rabbi
Ishmael, I shall overturn the world."

Hearing that, Rabbi Ishmael would not speak.
He refused to cry out. Dying in silence, he saved
the world.

ALEH EZKERAH

The Word and the World

Speech enchants us and bewilders us. Language, marvelous and various, provides a window to see into our
minds. One who would know a community can find its

qualities in its language. Anthropologists tick off the differences in societies by noting the differences in their vocabularies, in their syntax and sentences. Language untangles the ages, allowing a historian to peek back through time, reading carved clay tablets hewn by ancient peoples who could not imagine a day when their concerns would survive in universities and museums. But language is not only an artifact. It is alive. Language overflows in the heated metaphors of lovers; it sizzles in angry exchange; it smooths and sharpens, ruffles and unravels, creates reality by fable, by concepts, by legends, and by lies. No medieval alchemist ever dreamed of a potion more potent than the word.

Sometimes when we are alone, we call out the name of someone we love, someone who is not there. The name helps fill the void. As children, we would repeat names of beloved people and objects over and over again, a magical incantation that we hoped would bring the person to us. But even if it did not, the name itself had some of the glow of its owner. We are wizards of the word, from childhood soothing ourselves with the names of those we care for, with the sentiments we need to believe.

When terms change, the world changes with them. When words ring hollow, things collapse. Sometimes one can follow the glories or catastrophes of an age by taking care to understand the fate of its words. Struggling to express the turmoil of ancient Greece during its ruinous civil wars, the great historian Thucydides writes, "Words themselves lost their meaning."

The ancient world understood the power of the word. Epic poems carried forth what our predecessors believed about life, stringing the central lessons of the age on lines of verse. In the *Odyssey*, Homer tells us that in each generation the gods weave misfortune into patterns of events for future generations to sing. How does history make sense? By being expressed in words, perhaps even in song, tragedy gives birth to verse and makes catastrophe comprehensible. Language orders the world, it connects each generation. Under the tutelage of the gods we learn to make speech from random circumstance. Homer learns the same lesson as Thucydides: unless words have meaning, everything is chaos.

Words remind us that others have been here before, that others have prospected the world, sifted through the dross to find nuggets of meaning and order. We cannot begin to speak from scratch, inventing a new language with each generation. Rather we use the expressions of our predecessors. Each sentence hides the influence of the ages. A sentence, the most simple sentence, is freighted with associations, with connections to the speech of millions who have come before, who have forced their own bit of meaning into the tiny package of a word.

This is why words defy those who wish to destroy all that was and begin anew. Words are powerful reminders of continuity. Emperor Shih Huang-ti, the same man who first ordered the building of the Great Wall of China, demanded that all books before his time be burned. They reminded him that others had priority. Books proved there was a world before he took the throne—that there would be a world long after his throne was remembered only in the pages of yet another book.

The emperor wished to keep other people out by building a wall around his nation. He wished to keep the past out by building a wall around the word. For he knew that words let in the world.

The wall to keep out words could not possibly succeed. For words are not just a pleasant addition to the nature of human beings. They are of our essence. To a great extent, words are what we are.

The Spirit of Speech

The second chapter of the Bible recounts that God breathed into the nostrils of man and he became "a living being." The early Aramaic translation of that phrase, from two thousand years ago, reads "Adam was given the spirit of speech." The ancient translator has seized on a point that would be taken up by linguists throughout the ages: to speak is, in some fundamental way, to be human. The very breath of life pours into us this magic elixir; through language we become living souls.

To be human is to speak. We speak to communicate to others, but that is surely not the only reason for speech. People speak to themselves as well; they mutter, cajole, berate, and praise themselves. Silent thought is not enough. We surround the world with sound, even in our most private moments. Scientists have noted muted speech in autistic children, which some believe is not for communication with others at all. Rather the murmuring is an internal cascade, for it is simply part of being a person to arrange things in words, to marshal speech to scout out the world. We all speak not only to others, but to ourselves. We send our voices ahead of us to probe into the heart of things, to grill them, to make the array of life comprehensible to our minds.

We should not be surprised that no group of people that lacks speech has ever been discovered. Speech is a universal of human culture, in every corner of the globe. There are many mythic tales about tribes who have never felt the need for language, but these are fairy tales woven by verbal people for other verbal people. To be human, in whatever variety or remote clime, is to use language. We may imagine, in the pages of story books, what it would be like to speak only with our eyes. But however deep a longing look or an eloquent gesture may be, for the suppleness, the complexity, the sheer vastness of reportable human experience, silence alone will not serve. Nor will mere sounds, or sighs; whatever characteristics distinguish humanity from the animal world, surely language is paramount among them. For it is a vocabulary that grants us the range of meanings we can express. As the philosopher Bertrand Russell once remarked: "No matter how eloquently a dog may bark, he cannot tell you that his parents were poor but honest." Though silence can at times transcend speech, specific messages require words. To be a person is to use some sort of language, spoken, signed, written.

Conversely, to lack language has often been understood as to be less than human. The origin of the word "barbarian" can be traced back to ancient Greece. To the Greeks, the language of their enemies sounded like "bar-bar"—a nonsensical stammer. Clearly these were barbarians, i.e., those who lacked speech. That "barbarian" came to mean a person without any cultivation makes sense. To speak is to be a cultivated human being. The spirit of speech is the spirit of civilization.

Yet civilization is not only speech; it is also silence. While it is true that silence cannot replace speech, it is the background from which speech arises and to which it returns. As every people has known language, every people has known silence. Behind all our explorations, after we exhaust ourselves in words, the silence abides, waiting for us to discover it, to return to it, to hear a message momentarily lost amid the sounds of our own language.

The Spoken and
the Written Word

At first a word was something spoken. Words were tales told around fires. Words were exploits and fables traded among the tribe. Wisdom was recognized, enunciated, and shared. It was a long time before words were written down. For thousands of years the spoken word was magic. It had power, vividness, it was tied to the timbre of a voice, magnified by a lilt, an emphasis, a pause. The spoken word is yoked to individuality, to gesture. It has the immediacy of personality. The utterance is inseparable from the utterer.

When a word is spoken, it has a momentary life in the world. In an instant the air carries it off and it is gone. It can remain in the memory, however, and it is in memory that words grow, flourish, thrive. Sometimes the career of a spoken word barely begins until long after it is pronounced. Then it takes hold in the listener, and remains. So wrote Emily Dickinson: "A word is dead/ When it is said/ Some say./ I say it just/ Begins to live/ That day." So began oral traditions.

For generations the great poetry, laws, and ideas of humanity were not written down. In societies where memories were carefully cultivated, the same words were intoned through the generations. Professional reciters, whose job it was to remember and repeat, became the vessels of transmission for our cultural heritage. The epic tales of Greece lived many times in the mouths of these reciters before stylus was taken to parchment. In words sung again and again through the centuries, the *Iliad*'s Achilles drags the body of poor Hector around Troy behind his chariot. Surely, along the way, subtle differences emerged, the story was elaborated, refined, perhaps in places dulled, by the memory and creativity of the teller. Eventually there was a way to guard against the inventive and imprecise human memory—inscribing the words on a parchment that could not invent or change. What is written keeps faith far better than what is spoken. One scholarly theory, indeed, holds that Greek writing was invented precisely so that Homer could be properly preserved.

Writing must have been strange in the early days when our predecessors, the Sumerians and their ancient Near Eastern successors, first glimpsed this magical act. For writing *is* magic, a magic so well known to us that we tend to forget its force. But we can tell how remarkable writing is to one unused to the practice from a marvelous tale told in *Mercury, or the Secret Messenger*, a book by John Wilkins, published in 1641. Wilkins tells of a slave who was sent by his master with a letter and a basket of figs. Along the way, the slave ate some of the figs. Upon receipt of the letter and what remained of the fruit, the man who received the goods accused the slave of eating them. He denied it, despite the testimony of the letter. He was then sent back to his master, and given another basket. En route the slave again ate some of the figs, but this time took care first to place the letter underneath a stone so that it could not see him and testify against him. Again upon delivery he was accused, and, in Wilkins' words, "he confessed the fault, admiring the Divinity of the paper." Imagine the power of a piece of paper to know the truth! Even without seeing him, it spoke of what had happened.

The messenger himself was dumbfounded at the omni-science of paper. Yet such is the magic of writing: marks on a page can tell the truth about us.

Writing carries messages across the ages. We cannot catch the original inflection of the author's voice, but an-cient works still speak to us of other times, of hard-won struggles, of defeats.

So which is a more powerful force, writing or speak-ing? The truth seems to be that in concert they are stron-gest, for words that are not read, that are not spoken in the individual mind, cannot matter, while spoken words that are not preserved on paper will shrivel in time and lose their power.

We toss words, written or spoken, into the void, hop-ing that someone will listen, that their echoes will sound in the senses of those who come after us. At times the words do remain, having gained a certain majesty with the passage of time. We can see this unique combina-tion—spoken words that remain, recur, and grow—in the following story that was written for posterity. In it the spoken word echoes to us through the written word, and there is a glint of the original, powerful spoken voice.

In the Bible, the great leader Moses is preparing to die. He is about to take final leave of the people. But first he approaches his successor to give him a private word of blessing. Joshua has followed Moses for many years and now is taking the mantle of leadership. Moses, knowing how formidable is the task ahead of his disciple, gives Joshua a charge, an awesome charge: *"Be strong, and have courage*; for you shall bring the Israelites into the land that I promised them"* (Deut. 31:23).

We can imagine Joshua's apprehension. To take over from such a revered leader, to assume such an enormous task, is more than most could hope to achieve. Moreover, Moses had been his teacher and his companion. Now Moses was leaving. Joshua must have felt afraid and terribly alone. Yet Moses has not completed his charge. As if reading Joshua's mind, Moses concludes: "And I will be with you."

What could that mean—that Moses will be with him? Surely he will be with him in memory, but Joshua must have known that. There would be nothing unusual about that assurance. Even the knowledge that Moses' words will remain would not surprise Joshua. Moses, in these final, dramatic moments, must have wished to communicate something new, something Joshua would not otherwise know. Is there another, a deeper, meaning to Moses' assurance?

To truly understand Moses' comment, we need to recall the bracing words he spoke to his disciple: "Be strong, and have courage." Those words must have rung in Joshua's memory. They remained with him. They helped him stay strong. And in the end, they taught him a critical lesson.

For in the book of Joshua, which follows upon the end of Deuteronomy and the death of Moses, we find Joshua on his own, leading the people. In the very first chapter of that book he prepares to take them into the land and speaks to the people of Israel as their leader for the first time. It is easy to imagine his anxiety. Will the people accept him? Can he succeed?

When Joshua has finished speaking, the book of the Bible that bears his name reports the people's response. They answer Joshua: "We will listen to you just as we listened to Moses.... Only—*be strong, and have courage*" (Josh. 1:17, 18).

The people used the same words publicly to Joshua

that Moses had used privately, in their last moments together. Be strong—have courage. Now Joshua understood; Moses would be with him in the voice of the people. The spirit of their leader would speak through them, and carry Joshua onward. The words of Moses would find their echo in the mouth of every Israelite. The tradition would not end with the death of the leader. It would survive because of the assurance the people had given. They would triumph because they kept faith with the past—they continued to speak the same words. What remains to us today in the Bible is the written narrative of this tale, writing that testifies to the power of the spoken word.

Words and Faith

Different faiths have approached the word in different ways. Christianity begins with the incarnation of the word. At the outset of the Gospel of John, the author tells readers of the drama to follow: "In the beginning was the Word, and the Word was with God, and the Word was God. . . . And the Word was made flesh, and dwelt among us" (John 1:1, 14). Jesus comes to earth, in Christian belief, and embodies the Word.

For Christianity the word became flesh. For Judaism the word remains ever elusive, intangible. Not incarnation but interpretation is the Jewish lens for peering at the world. For Jews, God remains invisible, without a form or body, and consequently God's self-expression remains intangible as well, unembodied, pure. Although God in the Jewish tradition would express will through words, words themselves remained invisible, powerful but unseen, the strange symbolic force that moved the world, but could not be touched.

Other faiths do not put this degree of symbolic stress on the word. In Hinduism, one goes not to worship, but for *darshana*, "seeing." The metaphor is visual, not aural. The Buddha's charge to his disciples is "come and see." One must see for oneself, and worship is connected with vision, outer and inner. By contrast, the Talmudic preface to most teachings is *ta, sh'ma*—"come and hear." "Hear" is a synonym in Talmudic Aramaic for "learn." The world is imbibed through words. Judaism's pathway to the world is paved with language. Come and hear—hear how sounds make sense of things; hear how a teaching touches upon truth.

In Judaism there developed an idea of parallel laws, one written and one oral. The written law refers to the Bible, and the oral law to the Talmud and Midrash, the ancient discourses of the Rabbis. The written law, which tradition envisioned as having originated at one place, at one time, had the static finality of stone tablets. The written law was the pronouncement of Sinai—lasting, monumental, speech solidified to perdurability. The written law, like its Author, was, is, and would be without change.

Scribes enjoined to copy scrolls of the written law understood the care that must be observed to maintain the integrity of the tradition. In an age before printing, each copy of a scroll had to be painstakingly transcribed. This practice is maintained until this day. Torah scrolls are handwritten by special scribes, each letter fashioned in conformity with an ancient tradition. The scribe understands his mission to be a sacred trust—it is the transmission, the duplication, of the word. From the magic hand of Sinai to the exacting quill of a modern scribe, the word abides.

In the Talmud, Rabbi Ishmael, who we have seen was in his final moments vigilant in his silence, tells Meir the scribe: "Be careful in your work, for by omitting or adding a letter, you may cause the world's ruin." One who knows the power of silence understands equally the power of speech. A word changed ever so slightly can change everything, bringing ruin in its wake. Of course, the reverse is also the case: a fitly spoken word, a faithfully written sentence can uphold the world. A well-turned phrase, the book of Proverbs teaches, is like "apples of gold in settings of silver" (Prov. 25:11).

Building on the Bible, the written law, the oral law developed, grew—it had the organic vividness of the spoken word. The oral law was the outcome of debate and dialogue, not of the solitary process of sitting alone in a room and composing texts. The oral law bounced about the academies of the Rabbis with objections, expostulations, wisdom, impatience, advice, exaltation—all part of the process of religious dialogue, of sacred creation. Words hurled about by sages fell on the impressionable and eager ears of their students. Through generations the conversations were refined, pared down, and put in writing. The remarkable vitality of oral creation was distilled onto a page of text.

In early times there was great apprehension about writing down the oral law. One Rabbi, Johanan bar Nappha, went so far as to assert: "One who writes down *halachot* [laws] is as one who consigns the Torah to flames." Writing was too fixed, its boundaries too definite, its resemblance to the original biblical text too close. To equate the oral and the written law was to risk destroying both. This uneasiness persisted over time in Judaism. Hundreds of years after the oral law, the Talmud, was completed, mystics argued about writing down mystical secrets. The Rabbis feared that writing would rob the law of its spontaneity, its possibility for growth and change; it might turn a teeming debate into a static discourse, a flowing fountain into a sculpture of ice. The Rabbis wished to keep the immediacy of the spoken word.

But speech, while fresh, is fragile. In a time of exile, of persecution and difficulty, the chain of fables and laws recounted mouth to mouth is easily snapped. Lost along with people of learning were invaluable traditions they had not had time to pass on to others. The Rabbis realized that much of the law and lore was in danger of being forgotten. Throughout the generations there had been notes, bits of arguments kept on parchment, people who remembered and recorded earlier discussions. Over time these sources were put together. Now documents sheltered the arguments of the Rabbis and kept them for later generations. The legacy of the past was safe on the page. The corpus of writing grew.

So Judaism came increasingly to rely on the written word.

Creation and Destruction

Jewish tradition is taken with the idea that God created the world with words. Meaning was spun out of chaos through the sentences of the Everlasting. Judaism has ever been convinced that the seed of both creation and destruction resides somehow, somewhere, inside of words.

In the Bible, God speaks to Moses out of the fire, and God's words are likened to thunder. These images hint at the awesomeness of Divine language, which has the power of overwhelming destruction. At the same time, God can whisper to a prophet, touch a heart with a soft word or gentle question. As the Talmud expresses it, concerning God's revelation at Mount Sinai: " 'And God spoke all these words' (Exod. 20:1)—All at one and the same time. Words that took life and gave life, words that stung, words that soothed. Words that touched all at once: Answering the woman in her travail, addressing the sea farers and the desert wanderers, those locked in the prison house, one in the east and one in the west, one in the north and one in the south; 'forming the light, and creating darkness; making peace and creating evil' (Isa. 45:7)—all this God's words accomplished at one and the same time."

Language, in the Bible, in our lives, has both grandeur and grace, the welling up of thunder and the lightness of wings. It can establish, foster, nurture. It can raze and destroy.

This returns us to the story with which we opened the chapter. Rabbi Ishmael had only to speak, to open his mouth in protest of his torture, to destroy the world. Words are granted this awesome power of destruction. But Rabbi Ishmael will not speak, and his silence provides the trajectory, and the theme, of this book. For words are ultimately the bridge to an understanding that passes beyond words, and after we have managed to say all we can, there can be a certain salvation in silence.

Rabbi Ishmael is a model not solely because his silence was powerful enough to preserve the world, but because the power of his silence was a result of the power of his words. Rabbi Ishmael was a sage, a teacher, a man devoted to language and learning. With each bit of spoken wisdom, the force of his silence grew. To attain the true strength of such silence, we must first make our way through words. Then our silence becomes not merely an absence, but a resounding statement framed in stillness. To reach the silence of Rabbi Ishmael, a silence that teaches and saves, one must reach past the words that fill up our lives.

Could we exist if words were stolen away? What is the real nature of this incalculable gift? What path wends its way to a silence that is rich, meaningful?

These were questions that always intrigued me, but they were also theoretical questions. The deeper I went into the Jewish tradition, the more I understood that in some ways these questions are fundamental ones about our lives, and about our souls. How language works in our lives says something direct and powerful about how we communicate to others, whether we can communicate to others. Whether we can speak to God.

Still, in some way, these concerns remained remote. In time, that distance was to change, in a radical and painful way. As with so many things in life, it is not theory but experience that teaches true worth. What I have come to know about words, about their mystery and special charisma, is the result not only of study but of an individual ordeal, a family tragedy.

To begin investigating the meaning of words, and the journey toward silence, I have to take a personal detour, to describe the genesis of this book and its concerns. What happened to my mother, and in my family, is the subtext for all that follows. Like so much of value, this was a lesson of loss.

TWO

~

The Language of
Pleading Eyes

*God's gift of the power of speech was as important
as the creation of the world.*

RABBI HAMA BEN HANINA

At the age of fifty-three, my mother suffered a stroke.
She had been in perfect health.

One moment my mother was able, poised, articulate.
Then she went upstairs, screamed out my father's name, and
collapsed. She spent the next two weeks in a coma, fighting
some murky internal battle to hold on to her life.

A blood vessel had ruptured in her brain. An aneurysm—like a small balloon along the weak wall of an ar-
tery—had burst. For years the weakness had existed, a
mine, a time bomb whose tick was each pulse beat. Now
the explosion came, and soundlessly shattered our lives.

My family would gather around my mother's bed in
the intensive care unit and wonder where she was. We
watched her, hoping to spot a spark of that inner light. It
was impossible to accept that she was unreachable. We
kept waiting, waiting for her spirit to spring back to life.

We would all, together and separately, go over to her bed, speak to her, sing to her, whisper old family stories or current news. We were counting on the invisible: some secret hidden healing, some far removed consciousness, might be at work. The blow had been mysterious. A swift invisible grip had wrung consciousness from her. Perhaps the remedy would be equally unknown, equally sudden and sure.

There were times when I would look at my mother in the hospital bed, unconscious, or conscious yet unresponsive, and wonder if disease worked on the spirit as it did on the body. Could a stroke ravage a soul?

For all of us around her, my mother's stroke overturned the order of the world. The normal patterns of life crumbled. Everything was different.

We talked in guarded tones and codes, and ended always in the same place. "Well, what if . . ." "Let's just wait and see." There was simply nothing to do, and the stillness was exhausting. It was a marathon of motionlessness. Sit, and wait.

The progress of my mother's illness was long and arduous, and, like all sickness, it developed its own narrative. Friends who came, friends who did not come. Doctors who were kind and doctors who were gruff and unconcerned. Moments of sunburst hope, days of horrible gloom. The comments of friends, strung together into a mesh of support, reservation, analogy, and similar experience—it all found its way into our tale. Major battles turned upon an eye opened, a word spoken, a face recognized. The other concerns of life fell away. Sickness consumes the energy of the family as fully as it overwhelms the body of the sufferer. Sickness is totalitarian:

it is insistent, omnivorous. It induces exhilaration, depression, and intolerable tedium.

A long illness resolves to episodes. At each step along the way it seems that to move forward, to get past this problem, would be total triumph. Long-range thinking is too difficult; stamina is the gift of a day, not years or even weeks. "Dear God, let me make it through this day" is the prayer of one in pain. So there are phases: there is the shock of the beginning, which gives way to the long waiting, the anguish of impotence when all one can hope for is the resource of the loved one, the unfathomable artistry of the doctor, and the grace of God, if God dwells in those small, forlorn hospital chapels.

Words gradually begin to inhabit the domain of disease. The sickness becomes a story. The narrative of what had happened to my mother became as elaborate and well rehearsed as any tribal tale. At a certain point any one of us could pick up the tale where the other left off. We had agreed upon a sequence, an order of telling. The story exists in part to master what has happened; we repeated it verbatim like children needing to hear the same bedtime tale again and again, never changing a single word, finding reassurance in repetition. There were pauses in the recitation for clucks of sympathy, nods of understanding. For the story also served to bring visitors in, to let them know how the scene was set. That was our collective saga, the total meaning of our lives. To hear the account of my mother's stroke was to know us. To share the words that dominated our days—aneurysm, stroke, surgery, ICU, coma, shock—was to share the experience that had suddenly swallowed up our world.

For my mother, weeks of coma were succeeded by a long, slow recovery. There was no dramatic moment of awakening, though at the initial signs of consciousness, we all became aware that the coma was lifting. At last there was some slight movement. Over a period of days, her eyes opened, she began to take in the world.

She seemed to recognize our faces. For the first time in weeks, my mother sat up, looking about her as if puzzled and vaguely angry that the world eluded her. Bits and pieces were familiar, but she found herself in the middle of the movie and could not grasp the essence of the plot. We tried to explain again and again, but her puzzlement was miles off, far away from our clarification. For all of us, my mother's helpless bewilderment was even more excruciating than her pain.

The nervous wait was to discover if my mother's internal mechanism would work well enough to permit outside aid. Would her own body recover enough to give the doctors and the medicine and the care time to work? It is a fearful lesson in helplessness. Before you lies someone you love. You know where the danger is and what it is. There is no way to reach it. There is nothing to do.

Nothing to do, that is, except to pray. Pray to the God of last resort. I prayed for the recovery of my mother, but with very mixed emotions. Part of me felt that it was treating God like the Doctor in the Sky. The philosopher Martin Buber cautions us not to treat God as an "it," as a celestial dispensary of gifts, as a Being whose purpose is to grant wishes, however urgent. I was not seeking relationship, closeness, intimacy with God. All the things I preached as a Rabbi slipped from my grasp. I was a consumer, a desperate consumer of the goods God is said to harbor—health, magic, miracle. Not for me the God of gradualness, of the slow natural cycle of earth. I was seeking supernatural intervention; the God of splitting seas, of thunder-crack voice, the all-powerful Deity with the gentle hand. I wanted my mother cured. Yet I did not believe that God worked that way.

I had seen too many sick people who deserved to be cured, who prayed and hoped, and who still died to have confidence God intervened in such matters. *"Olam K'minhago Nohaig,"* says the Talmud. "The world follows its natural course." God will not reach down and rearrange the processes in the human body to accommodate me because of the fervency of my prayer.

Still I prayed. Part of the craziness of desperation is taking refuge in long chances. Who knows? All those sophisticated theological views could be wrong. Perhaps God not only listens, but acts. Perhaps the heavens have not only ears, but arms.

I stood in the hospital chapel alone, praying. I felt an arm around my shoulder and looked to see my oldest brother standing there. He asked me where I was in the prayers. I told him, and we continued on together. Then we cried.

In the meantime my mother showed slight signs of progress as well as hints of future debilities. She was awake, and periodically alert. Her right side was immobile, and although she could make sounds, she could not really speak. It was as if her spirit was in there, trying to emerge, but it could not force its way through. The soul kept bumping up against walls it could not see, like a firefly in a glass jar.

We simply waited. The short-term goal was an operation to close off the aneurysm, to ensure that the bleeding would not return. Recovery was the province of the patient. The doctors could only handle recurrence.

About a month later (it felt like months; time hardly

passes in a hospital waiting room) the operation that finally assured my mother's survival was successfully performed. During the operation we sat in a small room with
other families, also waiting, also scared. The room had
magazines, torn and old, often thumbed through but
probably never read. There was a telephone on the table
next to the lamp. Each family looked expectantly and fear-
fully at the phone.

When the call came, and we knew she would live, my
body shook for an instant as though discharging electric
voltage buried in my chest. My fingertips crackled, and I
slumped back in my chair. We all cried.

Then, like someone waking up after being shot on the
battlefield, we wondered what remained and what had
been taken. Before we had not had the calm to appraise
what might be in the future. The struggle for life was too
immediate, too intense—it was fired at us point-blank.
Now we knew there would be a future, and it stretched
forebodingly ahead of us.

After a brief stay in a rehabilitation center, she came home.
Her arrival was a celebration for everyone but the honored guest. She knew she was home. She seemed pleased.
In her smile, in the way she touched familiar objects, her
awareness was evident. We hovered around her, anxious
for each reaction, waiting to see how being home would
affect her. Yet so much of the past was blank, so much of
the present a blur, that for my mother it was just a bit of
a relief, not the poignant rescue we had anticipated.

At first she slipped in and out of awareness; a woman
of great strength and sharpness receded from time to time
and dwelt in whatever pocket of remote hallucination her
stroke had opened up inside her. Her eyes would glaze

over and her behavior would become arbitrary, irrational. She was gone, far away, unreclaimable.

Gradually, through rounds of therapy, the ministrations of time, her own inner strength, and the almost superhumanly patient caring of my father, my mother began to reawaken. More and more of her soul began to shine through. The terrific nightmare was ending.

But what would she be like when it was over? What would my mother have gained, have lost, from her nightmare? My mother had been through hell, through limbo, through realms I could not know or even fathom. I wondered what would fill her hands from the hell she had lived through. What would she bring back? How much of herself would she bring back?

Returning from hell, she was not the same. She was aphasic, unable to speak, trapped inside herself. Part of the language center of her brain had been destroyed. Whatever magic bit of mind allows us to fill the world with verbal symbols was gone. My mother, who was a university administrator, a fund-raiser, a teacher, could not speak, could not write, could barely read a sentence. The stroke had stolen her words.

There were other aspects to her stroke: the emotionality that resulted in tremendous rage; the bewilderment and the pain of being betrayed by one's own body. But those agonies were small compared to the inability to explain what she felt, to give voice to what was going on inside. Expressive aphasia impairs or destroys the ability to speak. At times when words can be spoken, the ability to form sentences is lost. Syntax is garbled, the wrong words present themselves, simple expressions are mislaid in the mind and cannot be retrieved.

Occasionally a word would emerge, a word to explain the horror of her condition. Early on, after a good deal of struggle, she managed to pronounce something she had been trying to say for some time: "Prison." She repeated it again and again with a sort of mantric regularity. It became an anchor, as other words would in the future. Prison. Prison. Prison.

Prison alternated with a nonsense word, a common symptom among victims of expressive aphasia. For almost a year, "kisskove" served as the catchall for anything she wished to say. "Kisskove" came out in accents of anger, of humor, of tenderness. Sometimes it was absolutely impenetrable—what could she possibly mean? At other times it was not only clear, it was eloquent; the situation, the expression, the connection all gathered together to make one understand just how fraught with meaning "kisskove" could be. In moments of tenderness or fury, when words are just whips we use to lash or the cords we use to draw close, "kisskove" served as well as any other.

Realizing, at times, just how wearying it could be on everyone to hear the same sound, my mother herself would make fun of it, wringing a few laughs from a situation at once tragic and absolutely ludicrous. Gradually over time, the word became less frequent, and then disappeared altogether.

There was some space opening through the bars of the prison. A few words came, at first haltingly. Later, select words could be spoken almost at will. Each word was a triumph of two kinds. First there was the word itself, averting for this moment the frustration of yet another misunderstanding. Even more, each word brought a hope of further recovery. Each word might be a sign that more and more words would come, that the dam might burst.

Perhaps all the words would return. Maybe the internal army of expression just needed to break through whatever wall was restraining it, and once again words would come pouring out. Perhaps they were really stored in there, in some secret camp in the mind, preparing to appear. Change was not dramatic enough to inspire optimism, but it was significant enough to inspire hope.

Through it all, the tremendous expressive force of my mother's personality came through. Her natural vividness was not dimmed in the least. Unable to say what she thought, she somehow managed to transmit the notion that her thoughts were ringing, sharp, clear. Her intake of information was restricted, since reading was impaired as well, and her attention span diminished. The loss of words rarely happens in isolation, and along with the inability to speak went other deficiencies and occasional confusions. Nonetheless, her judgments lost little of their authority, and her shrewdness none of its bite. Could it be possible that someone so alive would not return to full health?

In the years since she had her stroke, the hope stays, but now it is chained to reality. Some words, some abilities have returned. Still the prison remains and the bars will never give way. Things will not be as they were, ever. And in that sentence is a concession, and an admission, that I doubt I will ever completely believe, though I know it to be true.

When one suffers a tragedy, the population of fellow sufferers suddenly opens up. The world is filled with those who have undergone the same trauma, but one never knew it. Suddenly everyone was close to or acquainted with someone who had had the same experience. Stroke sufferers, people who knew the terror of aphasia, were at once the world's largest community. We were contacted by dozens of people who had been aphasic and recovered, or were related to an aphasic and knew of someplace to try to find help. There is no nationality so abrupt, so unseen, and so ready to spring into action as the nation of those who have suffered loss—the vast, wounded totality of the human race. We were now part of the great tribe of pain.

We quickly learned how many others had lost words, and how each had dealt with that devastating loss. We began to see how much is silent, and how many are hushed in this world that is inhabited by language, by books, by signs and screams and rhymes and songs and letters and language. Out of their silence, many offered help.

Help is accepted, if at all, with slightly mixed feelings. Each tragedy is a private one, and part of the hubris of grief is that no one else truly understands, can fully share. "You didn't know her" was our constant refrain to sympathizers—you cannot imagine the enormity of the loss. The smooth surface of family life was suddenly, horribly blown apart. We had been a public family. As a successful Rabbi in a large congregation my father was always on display, so, by extension, all of us were. Part of being in such a family is learning early that one is watched, that appearance is important, that the flourish of competence and presentability is essential. We had sprinted through life with the practiced grace of athletes. Now we needed help to walk.

Sickness strips away pride. It is humbling. It speaks in gigantic terms of our helplessness. The feebleness is not whispered, it is written across the sky. Everyone can see it, and you feel the notice especially keenly in those who avert their eyes and pretend not to look.

Now "we" were publicly ill. Pity, desired or reviled, pours out on all alike. My proud family had to come to terms with the fact not only that we were damaged, struck to the core, but that everyone knew it, and there was no place to hide.

All blessing is heightened by watching its loss. My family was always involved in words; everything was a discussion, every incident an anecdote. Our dinner table was a parade of jokes, debates, disquisitions. Watching my mother struggle for single words, I felt shameless, like a profligate spender suddenly confronted by true poverty. I had spoken words as if there were an infinite supply. Always one more phrase to illuminate that which had not been adequately explained by the phrase before. I stored up books and conversation knowing that life spans were limited, but language was boundless. No end to language. Now I knew otherwise.

Part of that understanding came through the agonizing but necessary practice of guessing. When someone begins to speak, the range of topics has no limit. It could be "Pass the salt"; it could be "Socrates was a wise man"; and it could be "I love you." The scope of what we put into words is as wide as human interest and experience. A single word can make evident meanings which might take hours to arrive at otherwise. Charades, that frustrating game, is what language came to replace. Parents experience this with children who have not yet learned to speak: the aim is sympathetic understanding, learning about a person even though the person cannot articulate his or her interior. But children will grow, and their inner world will flower into words. It is a different challenge to understand an adult who has no words, to catch a glimpse of the complex, layered messages of a fully formed person without the signal system we all use to survive. The task is arduous, and sometimes impossible.

Words are the bridge we toss over the chasm between selves. Without that bridge, we can leap and hope; but more often we simply stay inside ourselves, on our own side of the divide.

My family—my father, my brothers, my sister-in-law, and I—developed some systems, but they were a flimsy garb for the real truth: each time my mother began to speak we prayed that her words might be easy to figure out, that our missteps would not bring rage, or worse, frustration and pain. Every wrong guess was an affirmation of the distance. You don't know me, you mistake my intentions. After all these years of being together, how could we be so little in tune? A correct guess produced a wave of relief that reminded us of the distance in another way—it felt more important to get it right than to listen to what she had to say. Her communication became a problem to be solved, not an understanding to be gained. Each successful guess was a crisis averted. There was so much riding on figuring it out.

The real meaning of the game, as with so many games that involve human communication, is closeness and distance. Each wrong guess is a renewed realization that my mother lacks that most supple, usable tool for closing the gap between separate minds, the tool of language. Each right guess somehow suggests that we really know her well, we can figure out what is going on inside. Guessing "You went shopping" and being right is another way of saying "We are close, I understand the inside of you. You aren't alone."

The one who guessed was a hero. Family member or friend, anyone who managed to understand my mother's meaning, particularly if the session of guessing was excruciating and anger-filled, suddenly seemed extraordinarily wise, perceptive, prescient. There are tales of great Rabbis and mystics able to read one's character and history simply by glancing into one's eyes. We tried the same trick, but lacking mystical powers we had to make do with insight and luck. As often as not, they were insufficient.

Participating in this process of guessing and coming to understand how hard it is to see inside another deepens one's appreciation of the sad certainty that all souls are fastened shut. The enormous misunderstandings among people who love each other makes it clear that the prison is shared more or less by all of us. We all know that most of what we think and feel in the course of an average day cannot be shared with those around us. The richness of our internal life is in terrific contrast with the poverty of our revelations to others. Watching my mother reminded me of how little we know of the internal lives of others. Thousands of thoughts run through our minds each day, flashes of feelings, intuitions, apprehensions, and of all of those but a small fraction is shared. In this world filled with sounds, the uncomfortable truth is that most of the vast pageant of human emotion and reflection marches by in silence.

Even in conversation, only a few of the many voices in our head find expression. As we speak, our mind races ahead of the discussion, thinking of separate, often unrelated matters. We talk about the weather and think of other things, trivial and important. We all have multiple voices running through our heads at any one time—lines of type showing briefly on the screen of our inner psyches. Of the many messages we send ourselves, however, only a small percentage are communicated to others. There simply is not time to share everything. We are locked inside ourselves. I watched my mother, knowing she had been somewhere else, that none of us could reach inside of her to understand where she had been, what she had seen, what she had felt and failed to feel. Could words, if she had them, have closed the gap? As it stood, we were so very far away.

Child psychologists teach us that as infants we cannot differentiate between what is internal and what is external. Infants think that parents dwell inside their minds. An infant does not yet know of the separateness that both aids our sanity and ensures our aloneness.

As we grow we learn, however, that each person is separate. When a baby first learns to say the magic word "I," the situation changes. For the first meaning of "I" is "not you." "I" am differentiated, distinct; you cannot enter inside. All the internal words of my life echo within me, reverberate in the chamber of my self. You cannot hear them. I can keep secrets. I am alone.

That isolation was etched into my mother's expression. At times there was a desolation in her bearing that showed she realized all too clearly that she was cut off from others. The lesson of the child was impressed anew on her features. Surrounded by those she loved, she was alone. Hers was the language of pleading eyes. So often, we simply could not understand.

My mother's attempts to communicate forced all of us to confront what she lacked. What had been taken away? Were we all really in the same predicament, caged inside the self, or were words the salvation, the trail out of loneliness?

At times when I watched her sit in front of the television, for lack of much else to do, a look of faint disgust on her face for the whole predicament, I wanted to tell her something. But all the words of reassurance, of frustration, of care seemed hollow. They were heartfelt, but too easily endowed. They were spoken from outside her prison. Yet her struggle with words, her prison of silence, was not completely alien to me. For the bars that were so stout and vivid in her life exist inside me as well, inside every human being.

All of us, in different measure, share the prison. Our partial escape is through language. Speech is the vehicle through which we seek to encapsulate, evoke, present everything inside of us. Rummaging about in language like so much flea-shop finery, seeking the word that will shine, the verbal bauble to display our feelings, we battle daily to make ourselves understood. Yet we recognize that words are brittle and imperfect receptacles of meaning. They distort, fool, escape from under our grasp. What I think is different from what I say, and that in turn is different from what another person hears. The more deeply we examine and understand the part played by words in human relationships, the more apparent is their poverty. To know the inestimable value of speech is to understand its limitation. Every foray into language, if deep and sustained, carries one up to the forbidding border of silence.

Sometimes we rejoice in the indeterminacy of words. What a delight that words can have so many meanings! Interpretation thrives on the ambiguity of language. Without it there would be no puns, no great literature, no great criticism. But what can one do when the question is not interpretation but an urgent personal need to reach out to others and *make them understand*?

The marvelous ambiguity of language was a curse to my mother. When all you can do is say one word, multiple meanings are adversaries. "Shop." For clothes? For food? A particular shop? "Shop." You need to shop? Do I need to shop? Did anyone go shopping? Is that it? Why can there not be one, perfect name for all things in the universe!

The inadequacy of words is constant, but never so acute as in moments of great feeling. When the feeling is pitched low inside of us, touching bottom, it seems so deep that it cannot bring up words that are adequate. In instants of deep emotion, we need to stretch beyond words.

No one who has struggled to express a full sentiment can doubt that, in Kafka's apt phrase, words are poor mountaineers and poor miners—they can neither soar too high nor burrow too deep. They can bring us to the edges of emotion, but there remains a plane beyond which they can never go. We pile words upon words in an attempt to sum up our experience, and still the effect is hollow. Over and over again, the potency of that which cannot be said overwhelms our poor powers of description. "You had to be there" is another way of saying "You had to feel my feelings, to be inside me, to truly understand." Language alone cannot touch bottom. In the desperate attempt to summon up the essence of emotion, words become not allies, but enemies. As the playwright Ionesco wrote, "Everything is expressible in words—except the living truth."

My mother's inability to speak heightened the horrible distance between people, even the closest. I watched my father struggle mightily to puzzle out the meaning of a simple message, watched my mother strain to communicate that she liked the color of his tie, that she had prepared dinner, that she had seen someone at the store whom they both knew. Each communication, however commonplace, was a struggle. The battle was not merely a battle to overcome the limitations imposed by a stroke. It was the tussle of two people, bound in two different bodies, with two different

minds, to use their common experience and knowledge and
love to understand each other. The heartbreaking truth is
that it was sometimes just impossible. There were messages
that never got across, sentiments that were ultimately not
shared. With a dismissive wave of her hand my mother
would drop the subject, and admit her isolation. Each moment of resignation when she sank back into herself and
gave up was a triumph for separateness, for distance, for the
apartness that haunts all of us.

There is a blessing that precedes the central prayer of
the Jewish worship service, the *Amidah*. It reads: "O Lord,
open my lips and my mouth shall speak your praises."

Perhaps the prayer is asking for the mechanical ability
to praise. Like every other function of the human being,
the sheer ability to speak words, to wrap our lips around
the syllables, is not granted to all and forever. To be able
to speak is a gift, like being able to walk, to work, to
think. Like all gifts, it can be taken away, or never given.
At the very least the prayer is expressing the hope that we
will continue to function as we were intended.

That hope is just the beginning. Because to open our
lips suggests that there is a special power, something that
enables us to speak words of importance and of depth. We
are asking God to open our lips in a way that will permit
us to touch something deeper than the shallow pool of
verbiage upon which we draw in our usual lives. We want
access to the essence beneath. We want to praise from the
depths. We want our lips unlocked. The reservoir of ardor
and intensity inside of us can sometimes emerge, even in
words that are fixed, printed on a page, that have not
changed for centuries. We appreciate the wonder of being
able to speak, and the horror of being trapped in silence.

Watching someone grope for words, not to perfect his

or her expression, but merely to bring out the most ele-
mentary messages and meaning, is a painful reminder of
the struggle of all human beings, dwelling as we do in
separate bodies, seeking somehow to understand what is
inside another. Words are indeed the bridges we toss
across the chasm. In rabbinic writings the Bible is compared to a bridge that connects heaven and earth. The image is apt: a book provides the bridge; the surest
connection between two realms in this life is words.

The Jewish tradition is a tradition of words. What we
say, how we speak, what it means to connect to another
human being—these are central concerns of the Jewish
tradition. Perhaps no other system, religious or secular,
invests such enormous power and importance in the spoken and written word. Perhaps no other tradition is as
painfully aware of the difficulty of saying what is inside
of us, or so liberal with strategies and advice on how to
say that which is otherwise locked inside. Watching and
participating in my mother's battle brought me back again
and again to my tradition's advice about and reliance upon
words. How do we understand what words mean to us—
and to those who lack them? How do people really touch
each other? How do they reach toward God? And is there
a meaning beyond the words some of us can so easily say?

My mother will never speak easily or read easily again.
Her lifetime was spent in a world that values words. She
was trained as a teacher. Now she will never ask casually
for the newspaper to be passed across the breakfast table,
or speed unthinkingly through a mystery novel, or make
conversation unpunctuated by long pauses, a painful
groping for key words, a frustration with her lot. It is a
fate she will not forgive and cannot change.

What follows is not about her, but it is about her

struggle. It is about what it means to speak, why we cannot speak the words inside of ourselves, and how faith can help. What words can we learn to speak that will connect us to others, to the world, to God? What is the inner, sometimes unarticulated, language of faith?

The language of faith is sometimes unarticulated because faith is not only manifest in words. A consistent undercurrent of this exploration is the way in which words point beyond themselves, toward wordlessness, toward a rich and deep expression of human beings that vaults beyond language. The meditations in this book were ignited by watching my mother fight to recapture the connections between her and those whom she loved. Her battles made speech seem suddenly something strange, difficult, wonderful, and perhaps, in the end, not quite as essential as I had first assumed.

In the Bible, in the book of Job, when Job suffers a loss, the first things his friends do are gather around, sit silently, and weep with him. They do not speak, knowing that nothing is more expressive than their wordless sadness. The Rabbis of the Talmud teach that their behavior is a lesson in the proper conduct of consoling those in trouble. First you must feel their pain. Sometimes the most reassuring message is the one that need not be spoken. Sometimes the cries that touch most deeply are those we cannot hear.

Of one thing I have become certain, concerning my mother's character in these past five years: whether she wishes to or not, even when she cannot speak, she teaches with silence.

THREE

~

Internal Words

Death and life are in the power of the tongue.

PROV. 18:21

Our first words sculpt the contours of the surround-ing world. Mommy. Daddy. Baby. Words isolate and make vivid. In a confusing and crowded world of objects, words highlight the critical items. We break off pieces from the swirl of events and name them, organize them, make them graspable. Words give us our first hold upon things.

In the Bible, Adam watches all the creatures of the earth march before him. One by one he grants each its name. Once a creature is named, it remains in our minds, forever fixed in consciousness. Those whose names are not recorded, like extras in a movie, fade from awareness. In memory we have but a partial hold upon someone until we recall his or her name. When the name comes back to us, the person takes on shape and form, becomes real to the mind's eye. In the book of Judges, when Samson's father, Manoah, encounters an angel, Manoah says to him,

"What is your name? Tell us so that when your words prove true we can do you honor" (Judg. 13:17). The name is the beginning of knowing, the possibility of trust, and of honor. The nameless are lost to our consciousness and lost to history. We save, create, preserve with the word.

Part of what we create with words is our inner self. Although we view our environment in many different ways, the world itself will not take note of what we call it. The trees do not care what language we speak; the sky is indifferent to our nomenclature. What we say does not change the universe. What we say changes the self. Sentences spoken inside of ourselves matter.

The most elusive but persistent voice in life is the monologue inside our heads. Our inner voice branches off into three, four, five voices at once. Sometimes it is impatient, easily distracted, flitting from one tangent to another, touching on tens of topics each minute. Or it can fasten on one thought to the exclusion of all else for hours, playing the same tape over and over, spinning monotonously inside our heads. Internal voices play in recurring leitmotifs or single variations, and as the medley of melodies together forms a musical composition, so the totality of our inner voices forms a character. Our inner voice changes; there are moments when it is weightless, swiftly darting, playful; at other times it is thudding, heavy, and insistent. Either way, the voice is part of us. We all hear it. We create it and are both its victims and beneficiaries. Composers, conductors, and audience all at once, simultaneously authors, editors, and readers, we beget our inner voices, and they in turn shape us. Part of living is to grow more fully aware of those voices inside us, and to understand what, precisely, we are saying to ourselves.

The Psalmist tells us, "When I was untroubled, I

thought, 'I shall never be shaken' " (Ps. 30:7). Later, when trouble comes, that inner voice is seen as arrogant, those confident words themselves displaying the insensitivity that hastens calamity. His internal voice helped shape his fate.

Words applied to ourselves define us. They can be cruel or kind, well or ill chosen, but they become a piece of who we are. As we grow older, words become locked in memory, an ineffaceable piece of our sense of self. People live with the words others have chosen for them, and with the words they have chosen for themselves.

If we could unlock the blocked and pained memories of our minds, we would find that guiding the voices inside each person are series of words. They are powerful because we have not only heard them, we have absorbed them, made them central to self-image. They are rooted deep, deep in that unreflective but self-conscious stem of our characters, the place that makes us start whenever we hear our name. Frequently we have forgotten their origins. Sometimes the word lingers from the schoolyard, from the home, from a friend, a spouse. We still feel them. They do not fade away. How we understand our own words and use them reveals who we are. "Language," said the poet Ben Jonson, "most shows a man; speak that I may see thee."

In the Midrash,* the Rabbis take the notion of Adam's naming all the animals of the world even further. In the rabbinic retelling of the tale, God asks Adam, "What shall

---

*The Midrash we speak of in this book is "aggadic midrash"—that is, stories and legends told by the Rabbis of the Talmud, and some by later generations. These legends span a long period and many different lands, but most have their origin in Talmudic times (approximately 100 B.C.E. to 600 C.E.) and were products of the Jewish community in Israel.

be *your* name?" Adam replies, "Adam." Then God asks, "What shall be My name?" And Adam answers, "Lord." God then declares, "Lord is the name which Adam chose for Me; it is the name which I have accepted upon Myself; it is the name agreed upon by My creation." For the Midrash, God's identity, too, is part of words chosen and accepted. God will carry around the name that in the early years of creation was agreed upon. For the rest of the Bible, this will be one of God's names. In a stunning reversal, the Author of all things has granted to a flesh-and-blood human being the right to designate the Divine name. This is not only the largess of the Creator; it teaches something about the way creation works. To make something, to understand something, to relate to something, is to find words for it. For Adam to relate to God, God had to have a name.

To name God is not incidental or trivial. In Jewish tradition, to avoid saying God's name directly, God is often referred to as "Hashem," which literally means "the Name." The designation is momentous. In the Bible, a name is reflective of its bearer. It is not an arbitrary label; it testifies to the true nature of the individual. Since no one designation could describe God, who is the sum of all things, God is "the Name"—all qualities represented. The summation of what we can know of God is a Name.

In moments of grief and loss, a Jew is enjoined to recite the *kaddish*, the prayer for mourners. In it one says, "May God's great Name be exalted." Why make appeal to God's Name at such a moment? We take refuge in that which we *can* understand and know. At a time when God's goodness and concern are inexplicable, when they seem so far away, we cling to that which God has permitted us to understand. We can call upon a Name, and so feel a continuing connection. I may have a sense that God is hidden from me at such moments, but I can still call out God's name, and a sense of connection is renewed.

The Name is more than incidental; it is essential. A medieval mystic, Menachem Recanti, wrote, "Before the world was created, only God and His name existed." That is, only God's essence, and the Name—the part of God that could be communicated to others. God's Name represents the measure of divinity we can glimpse in this world. Faith can be seen as the understanding and invoking of God's Name. In times of loss, the *kaddish* serves to reestablish relationship.

The story of Adam's naming God is rabbinic. In the Bible, however, God names Adam, and that experience of being given a name marks each individual. In the early stages of life we accept the names given us by those around us. No one is so powerful as to fully disregard the designations of others. Molders of self-image, names seep inside of us; we can close our eyes and mouth, but even against our will, we hear, and we listen. Words filter in against our wishes, even without our knowledge. Unlike God, we do not solicit our own names. They are given before we can choose. They remain long after we have learned to choose, lying so deep inside as to remain almost beyond choice.

To change one's name in the Bible signals a change of destiny. Abram becomes Abraham. Sarai becomes Sarah. Jacob becomes Israel. Each change of name indicates an inner transformation. What we are called, what we call ourselves, is inseparable from what we are. "Everyone has three names," teaches the Midrash, "the one his parents gave him, the one others call him, and the one he acquires for himself." While the last is in some ways the most important, the Midrash teaches that all three are part of us; the names others choose for us do not disappear. We all carry inside of us more than one name, and each helps define us.

In the Jewish tradition, the worst curse imaginable is to wish of someone *yimach sh'mo,* "may his name be wiped out." To obliterate the name is to obliterate the person, to nullify him. Conversely, to establish a name is to recognize, to validate someone. For good or ill, the treatment of our name by others cuts deep and stays with us.

The Words That Shape
Our Selves

Words do not go away. Insults stay lodged inside us. The taunt of unkindness remains, and the adult startles himself with his own sensitivity to ridicule. A reprimand takes root, and years later the adult is devastated by a mild, even loving rebuke. Anything spoken in anger seems unbearable, for it is rubbing against an early scar. Often the old words, ones we do not even consciously recall, count far more than the ones we hear and understand.

Words are in the catch of our throats. Sometimes a word is stopped up inside, stifled, unable to escape. Imagine a traffic jam there, where the words of the moment cannot get past all the difficult, painful, and powerful words of the past. Perhaps we wish to say "I love you" right now, but it cannot make its way by the "ugly" or "stupid" that we heard twenty or fifty years before. The "I love you," with its insistence on trust, its demand of vulnerability, its command that we tear open the tightly wrapped shell of self, is too difficult while other, distant words that seem to have grown during the years stand in its way. We feel choked. We *are* choked, because we have taken in words that we cannot get rid of, that we do not know how to handle. Terms harden inside, become taut cords strung in the gut and the throat. They will stay inside of us, at times calm, at other times corrosive, at times preventing our doing what we wish, at times preventing our wishing what we wish.

When God approaches Jeremiah to be a prophet, Jeremiah exclaims: "Ah, Lord God! I don't know how to speak, for I am still a boy." God does not tell Jeremiah that he is not a boy. Rather, "And the Lord said to me: Do not say, 'I am still a boy,' but go wherever I send you and speak whatever I command you" (Jer. 1:6, 7). God tells Jeremiah not to *say* "I am a boy." It was not chronology but vocabulary that blocked Jeremiah. He needed to disregard his internal label. When he learned to speak the words of God, and not the words of self-belittlement, he became a prophet.

The realization that words cannot be easily erased has always been with us. That is why in the Bible, characters shy away from curses and oaths. Often a character will not specify the punishment that accompanies breaking a vow, for fear of even speaking the words. Typical is the formula that Ruth uses in pledging her fidelity to Naomi: "Wherever you go, I will go; wherever you lodge, I will lodge; your people shall be my people, and your God my God. Where you die, I will die, and there I will be buried. Thus and more may the Lord do to me if anything but death parts me from you" (Ruth 1:16, 17). Rather than spelling out what her punishment should be for breaking the vow, rather than actually speaking the words, Ruth uses the elliptical "thus and more." Ruth's caution is indicative of a respect for the power of words that are spoken. She will not even utter a contingent curse. The words frighten her. We can learn a lot about ourselves from the words we do not speak. They too remind us forcefully of who we are, and what we communicate to others about who they are.

Early words shape our internal voice, the voice that whispers what we believe about ourselves. That voice is not of conscience, but of character; not of what we ought to do, but of what we believe we are. According to Rabbi Abin in the Midrash, before Adam sinned, God's voice sounded soothing, intimate. Yet afterward Adam heard God's voice differently. Now, said Rabbi Abin, it sounded stern and harsh. God's external voice did not change, but Adam's internal voice, the voice of his conscience, the filter through which he heard the words of others, changed forever.

Sometimes the voice is a product not of our own actions but of what we have been told. In small, persistent tones it confides its damning verdict: "You're nothing. You're always doing stupid things." So deep in us is the voice that we fail to recognize that it is not, in some essential sense, our own. It was shaped by the praise, the blame, the unkindness, the care of others. It can tell us we are unique, soaring souls, capable of wonderful things. It can teach us we are limited, incapacitated, failures. The voice remains from those times that are, in our own personal archaeology, prehistoric.

Amid the tumult of our lives we do not always have access to those prehistoric voices, although they continue to influence us. Only when we are stilled, when we subdue the din of the everyday, can we hear the descriptions and the epithets that lie at the bottom of who we think we are.

There is a rabbinic legend that if all things in the world were quiet for a moment, we would hear the sound of God's voice reverberating from Mount Sinai, pronouncing, in waves of majestic sound that roll down the centuries, the words of the ten commandments. The Midrash is teaching that the formative words of the world never fully disappear.

That same poetic image applies in our own lives. Early voices, godlike, never fully fade. Gentle, judgmental, warm, wrathful, their vibrations change the quality of our own voices. Even though the early words are masked, they persist, weighing, evaluating, comforting, rebuking.

Perhaps the early expression was casual, said without thought, tossed off and forgotten. The original impetus for the voice may have been trivial, passing. The speaker may forget, but the listener remembers. The insult, lightly regarded, can burn for years, can sear the soul. Words can indeed hurt as much as sticks and stones, bruising more deeply, lasting far longer. In the Bible, Job, who is suffering physically, seems even more hurt by his friends' callousness. "How long," he asks, "will you grieve my spirit, and crush me with words?" (Job 19:2). Wounds to the body can heal on their own. The soul does not grow a second skin.

Each person, with a measure of effort, could make a list of those words that are most burdensome, words that early experience makes difficult to say. For one who seeks to be invulnerable, the word "hurt" will not emerge. Such a person is always "fine."

Even when the facade crumbles a bit, one can be angry or upset, but never hurt, because that is too revealing of vulnerability. Steel has wrapped around the inner core and cannot be penetrated; but words that are not allowed in are often kin of others we seek, and "hurt" links arms with "love." Who cannot say one will never really speak the other. We may be able to produce the syllables, but not the sentiment. As God says of Israel in the book of Isaiah: "This people has drawn close to Me with words, and honored Me with its lips, but kept its heart distant from Me" (29:13). Until the people repented, until they softened and opened their hearts, they could not reach toward God. When we bolt a door long enough, fastening it tight so that no one can come in, the bolt rusts, and in time we cannot get out.

To seek God, one must be willing to feel need. In the Jewish tradition, petitionary prayers are in the plural. "Heal *us*," says the prayer, not "Heal *me*." Many reasons are given for this approach. Some say it is to train each worshiper to feel the needs of the community. Others argue that it allows us to bury our real desires inside of a general petition so that we need not reveal to others our true request, and we leave it to God to understand the secret wishes of the asking heart.

Another reason has to do with the education of need. For one day, after years of praying for others to be healed, one needs healing oneself. Then the prayer, suddenly, is about oneself. All those people who are reciting the prayer with you—they are praying for you! The plural has become personal. The grammar has not changed, but the heart has. This time, bowed before the sky, blessing God, the worshiper understands that the prayer was waiting, cloaked in its communal address, for the single spirit to say, "Heal me, Lord, for I need to be healed."

On that day, one's prayer becomes precious to God,

because words often repeated have finally come home to the heart.

All too often, words are used to fend off inquiry, to mislead, not to reveal. We learn early that words are our most potent tools to conceal feelings. So on the attack of inquiry—for any attempt to probe can seem an attack—we draw weapons. The redoubtable weapons of words.

Words are swords and they are shields. I will push you away with my words. Smiling all the while, I will, by formality, by politeness, by a kind manner that is miles away, set up no-trespassing signs at the outposts of my soul.

I will wrap myself in words, clever, obfuscating, complicated, sweet, smooth words, and I will remain unmoved.

Talk to me about emotion, and I will spin passions into arguments. Storm on, wail and upbraid; I will answer with an outline, with sequence, and studied disputation.

If you seek to touch me, I will diffuse your emotion with a joke. A pun will snap the edge off your concern. A quip will keep you out.

I will wash you in torrents of words, spill out conversation in buckets, cajole, argue, spin pinwheels of radiant words—so long as I do not need to speak those wrenching and horrible things, the difficult words, the ones that signal vulnerability, perplexity, loneliness. The kind of words we really would speak if we took the talmudic admonition seriously: "Do not speak with your mouth what you do not feel in your heart."

The block begins early in our lives, and is symbolized in the very clothes we wear. How common is it to wear kerchiefs, tight collars, bands around our throat that show how that narrow passage is so easily blocked? Why do men wear ties? Perhaps because so many men have knots in their throats. Each day we wake up, choke ourselves off, lodge a knot at the base of our throats, and only then go out to meet the world. The symbolism is so palpable it is painful. Whether we clamp down on our words with a golden necklace (aptly called a "choker") or a cloth necktie, we have kept the words down deep, where they are comfortably sheltered in shadows, away from the light.

This caution is foreshadowed in the very first direct expression of emotion in the Bible. Adam's words presage all that follows, all of the evasions, the aversions, the words that will not come forth. After Adam has eaten the fruit, God comes to look for him and for Eve. Adam offers the first honest response in the Bible. When asked where he is, he responds, "I was afraid because I was naked, so I hid" (Gen. 3:10).

Words of Fear

Some words we speak easily, but only on levels we can manage. Their deeper implications go untouched, because to plunge deeply enough into any sentiment is to encounter a bit of fear. To feel is in part to fear: to fear the power of our emotion, the depth of attachment, the certainty of loss, the uncertainty whether sentiment is shared.

We see this anxiety sharply etched in the book of Ecclesiastes. There are moments when the author is untroubled, but invariably he recalls the transience of things, both the unfairness and the brevity of life. His apprehensions may be momentarily calmed, but then some experience or recollection shakes loose the realization that fear and futility are always poised at the gate of human consciousness, eager to enter: "And so I loathed life. For I was distressed by all that goes on under the sun, because everything is futile and pursuit of wind" (2:17).

Each person lives with anxieties that lie underneath the surface of daily life but do not disturb the surface until moments of particular discomfort. The surface of life is untroubled partly because we have learned in infancy to trust. There are others who will take care of us and love us. But the vagaries of the world cannot be calmed by trust alone. For the world is too uncertain to believe that anyone, however loving or trustworthy, can make it truly safe. We dwell on spinning earth like the passengers on an airplane. People on a plane will eat and read and sleep, seemingly oblivious to the fact that they are magically suspended far above the ground. Everything is calm. But the calm changes as soon as the plane hits turbulence. Then the passengers grip seat handles, look anxiously around, check the eyes of others to see if they too are worried, feel the fear that has been lurking just beneath the surface, waiting to emerge. The serenity was just a show, a show in which the actors wrote the script and convinced themselves the script was true. Deep down, they were afraid. They could not allow themselves to feel the fear, for to feel fear can be paralyzing. If the fear was felt, no one would step onto the plane. But at times the denial is shaken out of us. At times every passenger remembers that the air through which the aircraft hurtles at hundreds of miles an hour is an insubstantial thing indeed. When the plane begins to shudder, the terror cannot be ignored. At such times, the somber perspective of Ecclesiastes certainly seems persuasive.

Like passengers on a plane, we do not usually permit ourselves to feel our own fear. But when life hits turbulence, anxieties break through anew. When we are sick, or those whom we love are sick, or someone close to us dies fears about the transience of life and the dangers of the dependence speak to us again.

At times we can reach to the heart of things through words. Each year, the *Unetaneh Tokef* prayer on Yom Kippur reflects on the coming year and asks, "Who shall live and who shall die?" By speaking the words, by compelling ourselves to articulate the eventual fate of all, we force our fears through and look at them in the light.

Facing ourselves, we are once again stripped and, as the biblical phrase has it, naked as when we first came into this world. That feeling of exposure leads some to hide from themselves, from God. We recall those words of Adam: "I was afraid because I was naked, so I hid." At other times, however, it leads us not to hide, but to seek; not to avoid Divinity, but to reach toward it.

Nakedness and Covering

In the Bible, one of the first acts of the human being, of Adam and Eve, is to hide. They claim to be hiding from God's anger, and the reader smiles at the naive assumption that cowering behind a bush will protect them from God's sight. Eventually the text reveals the true situation—they are really hiding from themselves. Having eaten the fruit God prohibited, Adam and Eve immediately seek concealment, first by clothing themselves, and then by hiding themselves in the garden. The full terror of what they have done is borne in on them. The story begins artfully with a primary experience of human nature: the practice of hiding our selves from ourselves.

That is why God's question, the first question in the Bible, is metaphorical, not literal: "Adam, where art thou?" The first question is the eternal one: Where art thou? Are you hiding because you cannot face yourself?

Adam tells God that he hid because he was naked. The Rabbis of the Talmud interpret the word "naked" in this context to mean "naked of *mitzvot*"—of commandments, or worthy deeds. What Adam and Eve were really missing, and needed to cover, was the poverty of their own inner resources. They were denuded of character.

Many different suggestions have been offered to account for Adam and Eve's donning clothing right after their sin. It is clear, however, that these characters are confronting the painful experience of exposure, of nakedness, in a moral sense. We all understand what it means to want to "crawl into a hole," to hide after having done something of which we are ashamed. Adam and Eve are ashamed, frightened. We instantly empathize with their mortification at finding themselves exposed. They do not know how to talk their way out of it. Lacking the modern reflex of dissimulation, of misleading with clever rhetoric, they are helpless. Adam and Eve have no smooth words to cover their sin.

The power of words to conceal has just begun to dawn upon these earliest ancestors. Adam and Eve are not yet sure how they can best use language to hide their real feelings. Later in history it would become clear that words are the natural camouflage of sentiment. Later, the practice of lying would be brought to a high pitch of artistry, and people would keep others out by a well-chosen word. We would learn how to turn another aside, how to put conversation in chains. Soon human beings would learn how to plant a false world in the mind of another by the deceptive use of words.

For Adam and Eve there was much to hide, many internal weaknesses to guard. Although they had not yet mastered the language of concealment, they intuitively sought another means, clothing themselves and hiding. Once they have eaten the fruit, Adam and Eve appreciate a truth that follows their human descendants throughout time: to be naked, to be uncovered, is to feel vulnerable. Behind the curtain, unseen, we can pretend to be gods. We can be the great and powerful wizards of Oz. When the curtain is drawn aside, the pitiable truth lies exposed to view. Once seen, we are feeble human beings.

Clothing protects and hides us, makes us feel secure. Concealment grants strength, and the greater the disguise, the more complete the power. Superheroes in comic books and movies always wear a disguise. To be perfectly covered, to be camouflaged beyond the poor power of the people of Gotham City to know your true identity, is to be invulnerable. As soon as someone discovers the true identity, the hero is stripped, vulnerable. Omnipotence has been lost. To be disguised is to be strong. To be naked is to confront our powerlessness.

Thus we can understand another critical reference to nakedness in the Bible. In the book of Job, the hero endures a succession of disasters. After suffering the terrible travail of losing his property and then his children, Job speaks these famous words: "Naked came I out of my mother's womb, and naked shall I return" (Job 1:21). Naked came I out of my mother's womb. Naked—without defenses. Naked—without mistrust. Naked—without the powerful, almost impenetrable shell that we spin over our souls in order to keep alive. Since those initial days, Job, like all human beings, has woven an elaborate network of protection, involving social conventions and individual resource. Now that catastrophe has struck, it has stripped away all the coverings Job had built up to preserve himself in this world. He is back to his original state. All his stratagems and ingenuity will not keep him safely covered.

Catastrophe made Job feel his nakedness. Until that point, he had been well insulated from the trials of life. The Bible tells us he had been wealthier than any other man who lived in the East.

Job was covered, he was full of possession. Until suddenly, he was naked. And afraid.

Having lost everything, Job tries to use other ways to cover his nakedness, to protect himself. He discovers, as we all do, that there are many ways to be protected.

Throughout the book Job wears his anger and indignation like a fur coat. It keeps him warm. Having lost his wealth, he has little left with which to protect himself. When physical covering fails us, we turn to other coverings. In the magnificent speeches that Job hurls at the sky, in their eloquent indignation, is the one covering still left him. His dignity pours itself out in words. The story of Job survived through the centuries because Job chose the strategy of speech. He chose the word to keep him warm.

We have moved past Adam and Eve, for we know that language can be a rich cloak. Like Job, who wields a powerful fluency, we discover early on the usefulness of words as a means of preserving ourselves intact, untouched.

How many times have we made casual conversation when we are really trembling? But words can cover for us. Words can push the world away. They will protect us. Small talk deflects the glance that sees inside. So the fear feels very far away.

Truth can be frightening because it is a revisitation of meanings we wished to forget, realities we had long ago buried inside us. When the Jews gathered at Mount Sinai to hear God's word, after slavery, after the terror of the Egyptian experience, the revelation was not only for the people as a whole, but for each individual to recognize his or her own truth inside of God's words. Each one must learn in his or her own life how to bring forth words that are true and come from deep inside—this, too, is part of God's revelation.

Yet according to the biblical depiction, God's address from the mountain was not comforting, but frightening. Upon hearing God's voice, the people trembled with fear. They pleaded with Moses, "You speak to us" (Exod. 20:16). Why? This was before the sin of the golden calf, and God was not speaking in anger. This was a people who had known anger and the threat of punishment, for they had all heard the voice of the Egyptian slavemaster that portended suffering and death. Why should the voice of God, the voice of life and truth, scare them so?

More is involved here than the volume, the timbre, the awesomeness of God's voice. What frightened the people was not the blare of the message, but its meaning. We recall that revelation was not only a general message, but that it touched each individual, that each soul was laid bare by the words of God. To hear the content of those words, to have their inner being exposed and understood, to hear *words of truth*, was enough to make slaves afraid. The voice of God showed them the truths of their own being, the buried truths they dared not face.

The children of Israel were used to hiding. They hid
from the master's lash, and from themselves. Accustomed
to dealing with slavemasters, they were well practiced in
excuses and evasions. Slaves not only cower, they constantly mislead to save themselves another stroke of the
lash. Now slavery had ended. The first lesson was in
speaking the truth about themselves; in being strong
enough to endure listening to the word of God. They
could no longer hide. They could not be free only exter-
nally. They had to be free, honest, in their own souls. As
Rabban Gamliel said in a later generation, "No student
may enter the house of study whose inside is not like his
outside." It is not enough to have the external trappings
of freedom or of competence. Internal honesty is vital.
The former slaves at the foot of Sinai shook with fear not
so much at the sound of God's voice as at the sight of
their own souls.

The lesson that lies on one trajectory throughout the
Bible, from Adam to Sinai to Job, is the power of words
of truth spoken from inside the soul. Ultimately the splendor of the book of Job derives from the honesty of Job's
own statement about the words he speaks. Job's friends
insist that he has committed sins he will not admit. Job
insists upon his own innocence. Despite the pressure his
friends bring to bear, Job will not lie about his own conduct, not to appear pious, not even to evade the punishment of God.

Job refuses to conceal or pervert his words to conform
with the pieties of his friends. He says to them, "As long
as there is life in me, and God's breath is in my nostrils,
my lips will speak no wrong, nor my tongue utter deceit.
Far be it from me to say you are right; until I die I will
maintain my integrity" (Job 27:3–5). His integrity lies in

knowing the truth about himself and being willing to speak words that reflect that truth. Job knows that words of truth are sentinels of the self. They guard our decency.

Part of the paradox of words is that the truth is so much more frightening than the lie. God's voice was more threatening than the slavemaster not because of its power, but because of its truth. Job's apparently blasphemous truth was more fearsome than the devout, ready-made platitudes of his friends. As the Baal Shem Tov, the founder of Chasidism, told a disciple: "In certain hours a glance can flood the soul with a great light. But the men of fear build walls to keep the light away." The Baal Shem Tov taught his disciples how to use words, in parables, sayings, prayers, to pierce the walls we build inside. Hiding, darkness, and lies sound fearsome, but they are the cozy niches of the soul. They keep us from the words we do not wish to hear. They keep us covered.

At times we flee from the truths about ourselves as individuals. We decline to speak words that describe what we truly feel, or what we truly are. Sometimes it is not individuals alone who hide. Instead we hide together, as families, as groups, as societies. We blanket ourselves in the collective, so that we all look the same, using denial and evasion as our common cloak. We use blizzards of words to achieve the leveling effect described by the poet Robert Bridges, writing of London snow: "Hiding difference, making unevenness even / Into angles and crevices softly drifting and sailing."

Words of the Group

We do not avoid words only as individuals. We avoid them as families and as a society.

Families conspire not to speak certain words, words that are too difficult, or too revealing. Like individuals, families must believe; they must believe in their collective stories, their collective characterizations. One member of the family is the kind one, or the clumsy one, or the smart one. Together the family is motivated or hospitable, warm or cold. Evidence to the contrary is dismissed. People cannot be permitted to change. Old animosities and old attachments are not revised as people grow. The names, nomenclature, certainties have become fixed. No one wishes to learn a new vocabulary for people who have been so comfortably filed for so long.

When in the Bible Jacob is about to meet his brother Esau, the brother whom he betrayed years before, he is certain that Esau means to kill him. For that is the Esau he once knew, and he cannot imagine the softening of time on his once fierce brother.

Years before, Jacob usurped his brother's place, taking the coveted birthright. Exploiting his father's blindness, Jacob pretended to be Esau, fooling his father and establishing the firstborn's inheritance for himself. As a consequence Jacob was forced to flee from home, to escape his older brother's wrath.

It is curious, or perhaps not so curious, that it was Jacob's voice, his words, which almost betrayed his deception. Jacob dressed in Esau's clothing and disguised his hairless skin so that his hands would feel, to his aging father, like the hirsute hands of his older brother. Isaac asked his son Jacob to draw closer; he suspected some deception. As Jacob drew close to his father, Isaac said, "The voice is the voice of Jacob, yet the hands are the hands of Esau" (Gen. 27:22). He almost penetrated to the truth by virtue of Jacob's words. But subterfuge carried the day.

Jacob secures the blessing. Later Isaac discovers the deception, but words are so commanding that, having pronounced the blessing, he could not rescind it. The word once spoken has its own force. And Esau, wailing bitterly over his lost inheritance, swore revenge upon his younger brother.

Now, years later, in Jacob's mind nothing is changed. Esau remains frozen in the image of a hate-driven, unforgiving brother. Esau might have grown, but the possibility does not seem to enter Jacob's head. Acknowledgments must not be made if the myth is to survive. Certain words can never be spoken. Since he cannot link forgiveness with Esau, Jacob orchestrates an elaborate parade of people— his children, his wives—to greet Esau, to try to stir some vestige of sympathy.

When they finally meet, the "savage and vengeful" Esau falls upon the neck of his brother Jacob and weeps.

Families have throats too, where the past gets clogged as surely as in the individual. At times it seems as though one repetitive playwright were working on the script, with only minor variations for time and place, throughout the lifetime of the family. The arguments seem not to change, the expressions are eternal.

In the Bible, Joseph, the son of Jacob, has infuriated his brothers. More than once he has demonstrated a certain insouciant arrogance, telling them of his proud dreams. Joseph is the star of each dream, with the brothers in subordinate roles. In the dreams the brothers pay him homage, bowing down to Joseph. Even his father, Jacob, takes exception to Joseph's conceit when he dreams that his father and mother too bow down to him: the sun, the moon, all the stars bow to Joseph, brighter than all the firmament. Jacob's anger is all the more significant because it is he who is partially responsible for Joseph's conduct. By favoring him, by presenting him with the multicolored coat, Jacob has all but ensured both the arrogance of Joseph and the hatred of Joseph's brothers.

Now the elements begin to boil over, and even Jacob hears in Joseph's dreams the haughtiness of his beloved son. But angry as Jacob is with his son Joseph, angry as the brothers are, Jacob is unaware that the brothers have come to hate Joseph. Jacob must have seen the evidence. He is told of the dreams. But he cannot admit it to himself. After all, in normal families people are not supposed to hate one another. All the feelings of rage or violence that might exist are carefully skirted, avoided. Perhaps the memory of what happened with his brother Esau, and his own unfairness, makes it difficult for Jacob to see what is taking place in his own home. Yet had Jacob only listened, he would have known. The Bible says explicitly of the brothers that "they hated him [Joseph] so that they could not speak a friendly word to him" (Gen. 37:4). Had Jacob been able to admit to words spoken and unspoken, had he *listened* to the speech and to the silence, the catastrophe could have been averted.

One day Jacob sends Joseph to find his brothers, who are tending their flocks in a distant city. He sends his favored son to fend for himself against the brothers who despise him. At last the hatred breaks out; the brothers plot to kill Joseph and finally sell him into slavery. Jacob might have known, but he has concealed the possibility of fraternal hatred from himself. He favored Joseph, intensified the brothers' animosity by his show of favoritism, but remained deaf to their muted outcry.

Jacob's inconsolable grief afterward, when he believes Joseph to have been killed by a wild beast, is tinged with the self-reproach of one who would not permit himself to see. His favoritism has set the stage for tragedy. Certain admissions are more painful than concealment, until the concealment becomes a tragedy in itself.

The plot has recurred. Jacob, who took advantage of his father Isaac's blindness so many years ago, has become blind himself. As he deceived his father, his children have deceived him. As he spoke words that were not true, his children have lied to him. The family cycle, the family tragedy, has repeated itself. The deceptions of the parents have pointed the way for the trickery of the children. In each case, speaking what was false, refusing to hear what was true, led to tragedy.

The evasions of families are writ large in societies. Societies, especially in the midst of conflict, but even in times of peace and plenty, can find that words and meanings escape them. Like individuals, some societies have been unable to admit fault. For some, regret for wrongdoing is impossible.

A brief episode in the book of Joshua instructs us in this mind-set, and teaches the ideal. Joshua has now taken over the leadership of Israel from Moses. Up until this moment he has been Moses' aide, a position of tremendous responsibility, but nothing compared to the overwhelming task of ensuring the future of Israel. Now, armed with the memory of Moses' words, the people's confidence, and his own faith, Joshua must prepare to lead the fight for the land.

Throughout his years in the desert, Joshua observed firsthand how difficult and demanding leadership can be. No doubt he has mustered all of his resources to accomplish the task at hand. He is in the middle of a war. His energies must be directed toward the ends of conquest. The people are concentrating on the battle. All these elements combine to give him a focus that can at times be narrow as well as forceful.

Near Jericho, Joshua happens on someone standing before him, drawn sword in hand. Instantly Joshua becomes concerned and defensive. He is, after all, the leader of an army. The text continues: "Joshua went up to him and asked him, 'Are you one of us or one of our enemies?' He replied, 'No, I am captain of the Lord's host'" (Josh. 5:13, 14).

Joshua has forgotten the language of transcendence, forgotten that this world contains things greater than the two sides of the battle. Anyone he meets must speak the words of opposition, must take sides. The angel—for the Bible intends us to take "one of the Lord's host" as an angel—is on God's side. He tells Joshua to take off his shoes, for he is standing on holy ground. Taking off one's shoes in the Bible is often understood as a metaphor for taking off one's own narrow blinders, for seeing the broader sweep and scope of things.

Joshua is at a decisive point in the war to capture Jericho, a pivotal moment in the history of the Israelites. Precisely at this crucial moment God reminds Joshua of words that surpass anything he might conceive. Notice that the angel's response to Joshua's question "Are you

one of us or one of our enemies?" is not "Neither one."
It is simply "No." The "No" implies that Joshua has been
thinking the wrong way, that his whole framing of the
question cannot serve. Joshua wishes to slice the world
into sides—for us, against us. But the language of opposition is too strict and narrow for God.

God will aid Joshua, but it is important that Joshua
recall that his words must rise above the confines of partisanship, that as a leader he must teach his society to speak
universal words to God. The state that will come into
being must contain a vision greater than simply "us" and
"them." The angel's "No" reaches beyond opposites, beyond division, to a higher unity.

The Power of Speech

Tales of biblical characters, bequeathed in ancient texts;
vulnerabilities, cloaked over by well-wrought words;
healing and hurt, which reside, as the epigraph to this
chapter reminds us, in the power of the tongue: all are a
tribute to the enormous authority of words, language,
speech in human life.

The double strength of language is both in its concealment *and* in its revelation. Expressions can act in contrary, equally vivid ways. From the beginning of human
history, we have recognized the awesome power that was
granted to human beings, the power to formulate speech.

Words do not only wound. They can magically con-
sole, inspire, vivify. As we hear words throughout life,
we are creating an internal dictionary of those terms of
censure as well as of comfort that we have heard. Words
we will then be able to speak.

The Passover Haggadah, the guide for the Seder meal,

tells us that each generation is enjoined to repeat the story of the Exodus from Egypt. "And even if we were all sages, all scholars, all elders who were learned in the Torah, it is still incumbent upon us to tell the tale of the Exodus." No matter how familiar we may be with the events, the words themselves carry the magic current of liberation through the generations.

There are words that soothe hurt, that help us understand loss.

There are words to stir souls, capture and quicken imaginations, words that give us wings.

There are words of all colors and hues, from each land and tongue and time.

Words are used in everyday speech to impart information. Most of the millions of words we speak are given to this critical task. But they can also create or close distance. Perhaps the most critical function of the word is to pull close or push apart. That is why, at times, words can be so hard to say.

One of the ways we can learn anew the meaning of certain words is by looking in the past. Like so much else in life, words have their fashions. Some years they come down the runway as if this cut and concept were never seen before. We applaud them; they seem an indispensable part of the intellectual and emotional wardrobe of life. It is hard to imagine how we have not seen their importance before. But the trend fades, the cut and cloth give way to new words whose glitter is not dimmed by recent use.

Religious traditions seek to concentrate on words that do not follow the dictates of fashion. Religion is not about information. Sacred texts do not compete with modern media in supplying us with the details of events. That which is constantly changing, which provides the diversion of a day, is the province of disposable texts, like a newspaper. Instead a religious tradition reaches for wisdom, which means knowledge of what is enduring in human life, that which was true two thousand years ago and will be true in another two thousand years, for however long humanity proceeds on its restless way. That which is timeless is always timely.

Words can last. They have histories, just as people do. Others have struggled to be able to say what was inside them. If we invoke Jacob and Joshua, characters who lived in worlds so remote from our own, it is not out of simple archaic interests. Their battles are ours as well. We too fight partisanship, the inability to break out of the prison of images of ourselves, and the ready-made word cages in which we put others. We also know what it is to be frustrated, wordless, mute with longing, betrayed.

The religious searcher should be a diver through the deeps of ancient wisdom, seeking to bring up to the surface those concepts that can illuminate life today. Not all truth will be discovered in what is to come; some must be recalled from what has been forgotten. The past spoke words that have been lost, which we must reclaim.

There is a risk in discovery. There is no guarantee that we will be comfortable with what we find. Sometimes when we uncover or expand, it hurts, it is disorienting, we cannot embrace the implications of the discovery.

There is a syndrome that sometimes afflicts people who are trapped at a great height. Having clung so tightly for so long, they cannot let go to grasp the hand of someone who will lead them safely down. The metal beam or sturdy branch has saved them, and so it alone seems the only possible salvation. The grip itself, and not its end, has be-

come the most important thing. That is the way we cling
to our worldview, to the words we speak. The grip itself
is what matters, and we cannot tolerate its being loosened.
An improved understanding hardly seems worth the hor-
rendous risk of letting go of the rigid, secure hold of set-
tled views. We will not pry our fingers off the bar, for we
can never be certain that there will be another bar to grab.
We may grasp only air. We may fall.

The concept of God permits one more easily to let go.
Joshua was wrapped up in his assumption that all the
world, and everyone in it, belonged to one side or another. It cannot have been easy in the midst of a war to
have that view challenged. Yet because he recognized a
God above himself, above even his fondest aspirations, he
could hear the "No" and understand what it meant. In a
moment he would return to the siege of Jericho. For now,
he dwelt in a realm higher even than the conquest of the
land—a realm in which all things found their ultimate resolution, their perfect language, in God.

That was why Joshua did not answer the angel. He
remained silent. For he recognized, in that moment, that
the only language which could transcend partisanship,
which could be all-inclusive, was the language of silence.
It is the one language that does not originate with any
specific culture or time, is not associated with any given
nation or creed; silence is the one language that is universal, and so most deeply reflective of the nature of God.

Despite his silence, despite his acknowledgment of
God's transcendence, Joshua must have been frightened
by the prospect of letting go of partisanship, even for an
instant, in the middle of a war. Life is a process of describing what we may safely grasp and what we may safely let
go. One of the hardest parts of this existence is that what

can be safely clasped changes. What was essential at one stage of life may be a hindrance at another. The independence of youth may harden into the insensitivity of adulthood. But the hand will not let go, because long experience has taught how valuable it is to hold on, how terrifying it can be to contemplate release.

Many years ago the American Rabbi Milton Steinberg wrote a beautiful sermon about enduring a life-threatening illness and finally emerging from his hospital bed. While he was ill he resolved that he would never take the marvels of the world for granted again. "I remembered how often I, too, had been indifferent to sunlight, how often, preoccupied with petty and sometimes mean concerns, I had disregarded it. And I said to myself, How precious is the sunlight but alas, how careless of it are men. How precious—how careless.

"I said to myself that at the very first opportunity I would speak of this. I was not interested in being original or clever or ingenious. I wanted only to remind my listeners, as I was reminded, to spend life wisely, not to squander it. . . . I wanted to urge myself and others to hold the world tight—to embrace life with all our hearts and all our souls and all our might. For it is precious, ineffably precious, and we are careless, wantonly careless of it."

Then he recovered. At first he was indeed dazzled by the wonder of things. He strode with a full and lilting gait through the world, drinking in the spectacle of existence. The sunlight was a wonder, the smile of children an enchantment.

Soon, however, he found that other things intervened. He had work to do, tasks to accomplish. He could not sustain the same pitch of intense wonder anymore. He

knew that holding on was only half the human story. So
he struck a bargain with life. He would hold on, but in a
special way. He would "hold with open arms." He would
be willing to grasp, but also to let go. To hold, but not
so tightly that life slipped unknowingly from his grasp.
In his sermon "To Hold with Open Arms," he beautifully
describes his journey to that bit of wisdom. For he realizes
that holding on to life, to wonder and wisdom, is only
half the battle. The other half of life is the constant letting
go, the change, the slipping away, the loss.

Easing the grip on our certainties is a taxing task. Many
ideas may prove uncomfortable. Prying open one's hand,
or one's heart, is a painful chore. Perhaps with some slow
encouragement, however, our fist will gently unclench,
and we will decide to grasp anew on to something important—some words that strike deep, some silences that
speak even more deeply than words. Perhaps we will still
hold, but with the possibility of letting go, with open
arms.

As Steinberg says so beautifully at the end of his sermon: "Only with God can we ease the intolerable tension
of our existence. For only when He is given, can we hold
life at once infinitely precious and yet as a thing lightly to
be surrendered. Only because of Him is it possible for us
to clasp the world, but with relaxed hands; to embrace it,
but with open arms."

The struggle to grasp lightly, to approach life with an
attitude of passionate attachment yoked to a realization of
its impermanence, takes time and must be learned. It is a
balance that does not forswear the marvels of the world,
but realizes that beauty is not forever, that, in the title of
a Robert Frost poem, "Nothing Gold Can Stay."

Nature's first green is gold,
Her hardest hue to hold.
Her early leaf's a flower;
But only so an hour.
Then leaf subsides to leaf.
So Eden sank to grief,
So dawn goes down to day.
Nothing gold can stay.

Things are indeed gold, and should be cherished, but with the awareness that the gold cannot stay. That is at the heart of Steinberg's lesson as well, and as we might expect, as soon as Steinberg has reached this point, he wishes to speak of it, to tell others. To tell of his understanding is part of his understanding. For wisdom means more than to understand. It means to frame understanding in words. To some extent, wisdom is not real until it can be expressed, until it can be made real to others.

We all know the compulsion to speak when we have undergone a remarkable experience or come to a stunning realization. The very act of framing truth in words solidifies it. We are eager to tell the story of what happened to us, so eager that we will snatch at those we barely know, grasp them by the lapels and force them to hear our tale. The lover shouting love from the mountaintops makes love more real; the philosopher has to put insight onto the page; the dying man must pull others close and speak his last, as though life were unstable and uncertain unless pinned down in final words. "Unsaid" and "unreal" are not synonymous, but they travel together in our lives. What is and what has been must be told, or are as if they never were.

Joseph's brothers hated him for his dreams in which

they, and their parents, bowed down to him. Of course, they did not really hate him for his dreams. They hated him for his words. They hated him for what he told them, for his hubris in recounting his dream. The brothers would otherwise never have known of the dreams. In Joseph's retelling of his dreams there is the suggestion that the dreams are real.

Dreams are a wisp, a slight scent of reality, so long as they remain unspoken. Had Joseph remained silent, the dreams would have been a vapor, and no breach would have occurred. But telling the dreams was a declaration. Once spoken, they lived not only in Joseph's mind, but in the minds of his brothers. They were no longer mere nighttime imaginings, but signs of unbearable self-regard. Having revealed his dreams, Joseph could not escape his brothers' hatred. His words brought the dreams out of the domain of his own imagination, and now they would upend his world.

Although there is a wise rabbinic saying that action, not expression, is the main thing, we should not underestimate the vital nature of expression. To tell the story gives the action reality. An often-told tale of the Chasidim comes to us from the Rabbi of Ruzhyn. He relates that when the Baal Shem Tov, the founder of Chasidism, required a miracle, he went to a special spot in the forest, lit a special candle, and recited a prayer. When morning came, the miracle had been performed.

Once, after the Baal Shem Tov had died, his disciple, the Maggid of Mezeritch, needed a miracle. He no longer had the special candle and only dimly remembered the prayer, but he walked to the spot in the woods and recited what he knew. Again, the miracle was performed.

After the death of the maggid, his disciple, Rabbi

Moshe Leib of Sassov, needed a miracle. He sat in a chair in his office and prayed to God: "Dear God, I no longer have the candle, and I no longer remember the prayer. I do not even know the place in the forest. But I know the story, and that must be sufficient."

And it was sufficient.

This story, recounted in many versions by many Chasidic interpreters, makes a crucial point. Not that action is unimportant—it is of the essence. But the word, the tale, the expression, is more than a pale reflection of action. Reb Moshe Leib of Sassov still knew something very important. He knew how to tell the story. To know the words, to be able to conjure up the magic of language, is central in our lives and in the Jewish tradition. Even when one is sitting in an armchair, away from the forest, without a candle, words alone can summon a miracle. For we notice that the miracle itself is not explained—we do not know the situation, nor the remedy. For the miracle is the story. The wonder is the word.

Yet we know how difficult it can be to find the right words, and to know how to use them. Sometimes the more skilled we are with words, the more we feel how they do not quite convey what we wish. A great master of words, Gustave Flaubert, described in his novel *Madame Bovary* how, straining to speak words of great significance, we often end up with hollow sounds: "The fullness of the soul sometimes overflows into the emptiest metaphors, since no one can give the exact measure of his needs, nor of his conceptions, nor of his sorrows; for human speech is like a cracked tin kettle, on which we hammer out tunes to make bears dance when we long to move the stars."

We all long to move the stars, to find our way to the

heart of things. We all seek the language that can help us begin to search. If it is hard for Flaubert to convey the fullness of feeling, what are the rest of us to do, who do not have his legendary literary powers? Can a religious tradition teach us how to use words to deepen, to connect, to understand?

Judaism believes that such teaching is both possible and vital. Language is at the very center of its message. Judaism's teaching is how to bring us out of our silence into words that connect us with God. And then, once we have learned to speak, how to learn silence in a new way, a silence that also connects, a silence that communicates.

Perhaps that is why the story of the greatest figure of the Jewish tradition is also a story about the mastery of words. The story of a hero, it is a narrative that begins and ends in silence. In between it relates one of the most dramatic, poignant, and important tales Judaism has to offer: the story of the prophet who learned to speak.

FOUR

~

The Man Who Learned
to Speak

Who gives man speech? Is it not I, the Lord?

EXOD. 4:11

M oral currents of the world are carried along on stories. From the fables of youth to the anecdotes of
adulthood, we interpret the world around us by telling
tales. Stories do more than describe what was; they explain what is, and what should be. "Once upon a time"
is about our time too, and every fairy tale is a contemporary report. As the Latin proverb has it, "If you change
the name, the story is about you."

That is why the Bible is filled with the doings of people, and even the law is framed by narrative. At times the
dramatic story of a single life can bring truth home more
powerfully than any abstract description.

There is a sustained tale woven through the Bible that
dramatizes the ambiguity and power of words in the life
of a single remarkable individual. It is the story of a great
figure confronted with a great challenge. He has to over-

come, to learn, and through that learning to grow. The growth is not without pain, and the learning is not without loss. The story limns for us the true nature of a hero, far removed from the simple modern image of incomparable strength and emotional invulnerability. In order to understand this hero, however, we must pause to remind ourselves of some of the different models of a hero, for confusion about heroes and uncertainty about true strength are a legacy of our times.

The Image of a Hero

Images of heroism stir emulation: watching the hero, we wish to be as strong, passionate, grand as the depiction on the page or the screen. Sometimes the effect is so powerful that the characters in fiction seem more real and more worthy of emulation than the heroes of real life. Tragedy trapped on celluloid can be more vivid than anything outside the theater, where lines are not scripted and action is unrehearsed. Often the hero in the book or the movie really can change our lives: fantasy sweeps us into its reality, and we find the best in ourselves that corresponds to the imaginary images we revere.

As individuals and as a society we adopt the manner, the priorities, of our invented heroes. Their expressions become our clichés. Children adopt the tone and mannerisms of characters on television, and their parents, while at times seeking more sophisticated models, are also captured by the color and vivacity of fictional personalities.

The problem is that heroes conflict, and so we are never sure whom we should take as our own. One movie holds up a model of wit, flash, and grace; the next promotes quiet, unassuming strength; and the third exalts a muscled gladiator. We are caught in the midst of all these larger-than-life figures, trying to unscramble the ideal so that we might better live our lives and be proud of ourselves.

Too often our hero is simply the one portrayed in the last gripping movie we have seen, book we have read, story we have been told. Since our ideals shift, we identify with very different heroes, as long as they have something of the verve and fire that excite us. In one story we identify with the detective, in the next with the thief. Any character with the moxie to take risks, anyone who moves with style, panache, who has a certain carelessness and assurance—such a character will seem glorious. Who would not wish to be that way? What self does not want to expand to draw in more vital energies, to display the dash and brio of the hero?

Adults feel this pull, but in childhood it is everything. Having so little sense as yet of what we are, as children we are searching for a powerful identity to step into and become. Sports heroes, superheroes, figures from literature and myth—all seem to reflect the way we truly feel inside, what we wish desperately to be.

In his book *The Gentleman and the Jew*, the writer and cultural critic Maurice Samuel recalls the conflicts over the role models of his youth. He tells of having grown up in England, where the ideal was the gentleman. The gentleman represented a particular type of hero. The type was fashioned in part by Shakespeare, Browning, Byron; by literature and myth. The gentleman was the man who saw life as a quintessential game, who valued style and poise above all. The gentleman was the one who might lose the sword fight and with it his life, but he would die with aplomb: the gentleman would "expire" with a smile and a witty epigram on his lips. Life above all was suavity, grace, the elegance of emotional control and ironic detachment. The gentleman hero had ideals and took them seriously, but was never too solemn, too somber. The besetting sin of this world was less evil or immorality than being a "bad sport." Earthly existence was a game, and prowess was everything. For the young Samuel, the image, closer to an Errol Flynn movie than to real life, was enormously attractive and captured his imagination.

In competition with this was the far less riveting image of the Jew. Judaism was Samuel's own ethnic inheritance. He pictured the Jew as a gnarled, hunched-over figure, dressed in black, face obscured by a long beard, walking swiftly through the streets of London. The Jew's world was the house of study, not the gangplank or castle court-yard. He spent his time jousting only with law and legend, with arguments, with words. To a young man, the Jew was a poor model for a heroic image—indeed, it was not a heroic image at all. Next to the gentleman, the Jew seemed utterly uninteresting. Wrangling over texts ap-peared pale and irrelevant to a young, vigorous man.

Yet as he grew, Samuel noticed something about his lackluster compatriots. There was a knowing sparkle in those older eyes. They lacked lightness, but they had its opposite, a certain gravity, a depth. The Jews from whom he had sprung took life not as a game, but as a holy en-terprise. The aim of life was sanctity, not savoir faire. In the houses of study, where Jews pored over ancient books and sacred tomes, words, not swords, were indeed the real weapons for living. Eventually, Samuel gave his allegiance to the image of the Jew, whose heroism loomed larger over time.

For most of us, heroism is an attribute of action. Like the young Maurice Samuel, we assume that a hero is one who can manage feats of physical courage and stamina that astound others. The hero in the movies is distinguished by the ability to dispatch enemies, to confound the laws of physics and probability. This is greatness in the mode of the biblical Samson, a hero defined not by character, but by physical power, bodily courage.

Although we recognize the existence of emotional and spiritual courage, these are less often the attributes we associate with heroism. They are harder to portray. Constancy does not quicken the blood. It requires more attention to discern the gallantry of integrity. At times we are confronted with it, and we understand and applaud it. More often, however, the daily, steady application of an ideal to a life does not capture our admiring attention.

What is true heroism? In all the welter of conflicting ideals, can we settle on a single definition? Is it great physical power, or strength of will?

Giving two examples, the Talmud elaborates on the nature of heroism: one text teaches that the hero is one who makes a friend of an enemy. This is strength of resolve and personality, apart from any physical trait. In the same vein, the Talmud teaches that a hero is one who can master his own desires. Again, the heroism is different from valor in combat. It is self-understanding and self-mastery. Physical strength alone can be heroic only if it is properly used, and that requires discernment and wisdom.

The understanding of heroism is vital because what we are is partly shaped by an ideal image of what we wish to be. If you wish to know someone's character, ask about his or her heroes. What Maurice Samuel became in his life—a writer, a teacher, a champion of religious values— was a function of what he chose as his own model of heroism. In the central code of Jewish law, the *Shulchan*

Arukh, the opening phrase reads: "Each morning one should arise heroic as a lion to do the will of God." Heroism is embodied in goodness, in making life better, in bringing divinity to an often benighted world.

Even the solitary Jewish holiday that celebrates success in warfare, Chanukkah, has a message not of physical courage, but of spiritual self-mastery. Indeed, the word for a hero, *gibbor*, with undercurrents of might and muscle, is applied not to the Maccabees themselves, but to their enemies! In the prayer *Al Hanissim* ("On the Miracles") we are told that the *gibborim*, the strong, were given unto the hands of the *chalashim*, the weak. Heroism was not with the powerful and classically heroic, but with the weak who proved strong in faith and fidelity. That is why the verse associated with Chanukkah in the Jewish tradition is the following, taken from the book of Zechariah (4:6): "Not by might, nor by power, but by My spirit, said the Lord." Chanukkah is a lesson in the triumph over greater forces by those who were stalwart in spirit.

We learn this lesson because of the prophet Zechariah. It is not coincidental that these words were spoken by a prophet. The prophet is the quintessential Jewish hero, the hero of the moral word. Prophecy usually begins in the Bible with the declaration "And the word of the Lord came to . . ." For some prophets the experience is so overwhelming that it is unthinkable not to pronounce the word of God: "A lion has roared, who can but fear? My Lord God has spoken, who can but prophesy?" (Amos 3:8).

The word is so precious that it must not be lost. The great prophet Jeremiah had all of his prophecies, his life's work, written in a single scroll. In his passion for justice, Jeremiah was often critical of the ruling powers, and he prophesied that the land would be destroyed. When King

Jehoiakim heard of Jeremiah's writings, he had the scroll seized, cut up, and section by section consigned to fire. Everything Jeremiah had said, believed, and struggled for was destroyed.

Perhaps, had Jeremiah not been a prophet, he would have given in to despair. But he knew that the words he spoke had within them the promise of immortality. So, "Jeremiah got another scroll and gave it to the scribe Baruch, son of Neriah. And at Jeremiah's dictation, he wrote in it the whole text of the scroll that King Jehoiakim of Judah had burned" (Jer. 36:32). To be a prophet is to understand, to absorb, and to not abandon the word.

For the greatest of the prophets, understanding the importance of words was a product of struggle, and a story of triumph.

Transformation of a Hero

At the heart of the Bible is the story of a man who gradually learns what it is to be a leader, to be a hero, and it has to do with learning *not* to act. One who wishes to understand the importance of words can do no better than to peek into the remarkable transformation undergone by Moses in the Bible. Although action is very important in his life and legacy, beginning in infancy, another theme winds slowly and stirringly through Moses' life: Moses is the man who learns how to speak.

The struggle begins before his birth. The opening drama in Moses' life is a decree of death by the word of Pharaoh, who has come to fear that the growth of the Jews will pose a threat to his regime: "Then Pharaoh charged all his people, saying, 'Every boy that is born you shall throw into the Nile' " (Exod. 1:22). Those words will determine the course of Moses' life, and the future arena of his conflicts.

The theme of his life is suggested shortly after birth. Moses' first appearance in the Bible hints at his future struggles. After he is born, Moses' mother places him in a basket by the riverbank in an attempt to hide him from the authorities and thus save his life. Rather than being cast into the Nile as Pharaoh's decree mandates, Moses is gently placed on the bank of the Nile in a small basket that, his mother hopes, will somehow keep him safe. She succeeds in an unexpected way.

For Moses is found, but he is found by Pharaoh's own daughter, who has come down to the Nile to bathe. She spies the basket, and sends her slave girl to fetch it. When Pharaoh's daughter opens the basket, she finds the infant crying. There are distinctive features of that cry that we will explore more fully in a later chapter. For now it is enough to note that the text reads that Pharaoh's daughter noticed the basket, and that she opened it and *saw* a crying child. The text never says that she *heard* the cry, rather that she saw it. It is a curious cry that one sees but cannot hear. Traditional commentators have noted the difficulty and proposed various explanations. Perhaps the verse intends to be obscure, because it is foreshadowing a preoccupation of Moses' throughout his life.

What we can detect is a hint of something that the Bible will develop with clarity as the story proceeds. The trouble is with words. Moses is one who, from the beginning of his life, had some obscure trouble with articulation, with giving vent to his thoughts and feelings. Obviously an infant could not speak, but the cry one cannot hear betokens something larger, more comprehensive. From these first moments, there is strain in the way Moses seeks to communicate. This great leader begins as a child who does not know, according to the careful and curious phrasing of the Bible, how properly to cry. He is a child of slaves, rescued by royalty, who soundlessly weeps. He will develop into an adult confounded and discomfited by the need for language. The beginning of Moses' story is in silence. The direction of his life is set by this first, silent cry.

For many years after the rescue, until he is grown, we hear not a single word from Moses. The Bible does not describe the experience of this alien youngster growing up as the ward of Pharaoh's daughter amid the splendor of the royal palace. His childhood is shrouded in secrecy: despite all the marvels and curiosities that Moses must have seen being raised in the house of Pharaoh, the Bible records not a single word from Moses' mouth. His coming of age is wrapped in silence.

After Moses emerges from the palace, we become immediately aware of his reluctance to speak. Having now grown up, Moses goes out into Egyptian society. He is greeted by the sights of suffering: he sees an Egyptian taskmaster beating a slave. The natural reaction to this injustice would be to cry out, to implore the taskmaster to stop. But Moses does not speak. His silence remains unbroken. Rather his instant response is one of action, of violence. He strikes and kills the Egyptian slavemaster. Moses did not call out, shout, cry for help—he is one who saves by deed. This is a quintessential man of action.

This same scenario is repeated after Moses has run away to Midian. There, too, he wordlessly saves the daughters of Jethro from some shepherds who drove them from the wells. Again Moses resorts immediately to action. No dialogue is recorded.

We should note that in between these two incidents
Moses makes his first attempt to accomplish something
by speech, and he fails. After the incident with the Egyptian slavemaster, Moses sees two Hebrew slaves in a
brawl. Since both are slaves, Moses tries to reason with
them, to persuade them not to add to their troubles by
fighting with each other: "Why," he asks, "do you strike
your fellow?" (Exod. 2:13). They merely resent his inter-
ference, reinforcing the lesson of Moses' life thus far—it
is action, not words, that matters in this world.

Now living in Midian (he has run away out of fear
that he will be executed for killing the Egyptian slavemaster), Moses becomes a shepherd. At the momentous
scene of his summons to leadership, Moses is charged with
the task of leading the Israelite people. God calls upon
Moses at the burning bush in the desert, a bush that is on
fire, though its leaves and branches are not consumed.
While marveling at the sight, Moses hears the voice of
God commanding him to go to Pharaoh and demand the
deliverance of the Israelites. Moses tries various stratagems to escape. He does not want to be the prophet. It is
a monumental task, one that will demand enormous res-
ervoirs of will and perseverance, one that will find him
buffeted and betrayed. The prophets in the Bible are predictably resented and mistreated. An essential part of their
task is to rebuke the people. On the deepest level of moral
seriousness, the prophet is a scold. No one would will-
ingly choose such a life. Perhaps God chose the symbolism of the burning bush to reassure Moses, as a hint that
he would be a prophet whose life would resemble that
symbol—Moses would be on fire with faith, but his faith
would not consume him.

Yet Moses is afraid of more than the travail of a

prophet's life. He feels inadequate. He confesses to a sense of incapacity and provides us with the first direct glimpse of the problematic relationship of this prophet to words and language. Moses cries out to God that he is inarticulate: "I am heavy of speech, and heavy of tongue" (Exod. 4:10). That is the literal translation of a Hebrew phrase indicating some sort of speech impediment. Moses beseeches God not to force him to speak. As readers, we are not surprised that language is an obstacle to Moses. We have already noted his immediate response in times of crisis—a response of action. Paradoxically for this brave man, speech is terrifying.

Moses' speech impediment gave rise to a famous rabbinic legend that recalls Moses' upbringing in the palace. The Rabbis recount that a fearful Pharaoh, worried that this strange child would grow up to supplant him, conducted a test. At some distance from each other, he placed on the ground his own kingly crown and a hot coal. Positioning the infant between them, he waited to see which would attract him. Had Moses moved to the crown, Pharaoh would have taken it as a sign that the child would eventually covet the kingship, and he would have ordered the infant killed.

As any child would be, Moses was attracted to the twinkling jewels in the crown. However, at the last instant an angel came down and forced him toward the coal. Moses touched the coal and burned his hand. Instantly he raised his hand to his mouth and burned his mouth. It was this incident, according to the midrash, that impeded Moses' speech.

The legend has behind it the notion that it was part of a necessary design, planned early in his life, for Moses to be inarticulate. His disability was in some sense providential. For Moses to face problems in speaking would prove to be important. His encounter with God at the burning bush has been prepared, and even his excuses are a harbinger of important developments to come.

For in desperation, trying to fend off the mission, Moses pleads with God: "I have never been a man of words, either in times past or now that You have spoken to Your servant; I am heavy of speech, and heavy of tongue" (Exod. 4:10). Moses explains that his discomfort with words has been lifelong, just as the story of the crown and the coal would have it.

Moses says that he is not a man of *devarim*—the Hebrew term he uses for "words." He complains to God that Pharaoh will not believe him. Moses worries that as a leader he will not be able to summon the requisite eloquence. Why should Pharaoh credit this stammering shepherd? He is realistic enough to know that he is not the man to choose for the smooth diplomatic language needed to carry off the subtle hints and veiled threats that are the stuff of leadership. Moses' personality up to now has been a blunt instrument. He has a sense of justice, but not a sense of nuance or of language.

Yet God will not take no for an answer. Moses does not get to decide his own fate, or even his own limitations. "Who gives man speech?" asks God. "Who makes him dumb or deaf, seeing or blind? Is it not I, the Lord?" (Exod. 4:11). The point is unanswerable. God is responsible for Moses' attributes and limitations and has chosen Moses in full awareness of what they are. Eventually, Moses is forced to back down and do as God wishes.

This is the setup to a long and remarkable education. The prophet has been chosen, and now he will be shaped. As the tale proceeds, the Bible shows the subtle process of Moses' awakening. Gradually Moses becomes the man who not only learns to speak, but in an unparalleled way learns the value, the import, and the sanctity of words.

Mission and Fulfillment

Moses' first action as leader is to speak to Pharaoh. Since he is afraid—not so much of Pharaoh as of speech itself— he has brought his older brother Aaron to be a spokesman. As Moses anticipated, Pharaoh disregards the plea. There is no reason for a powerful monarch to listen to this scion of slaves. This rejection begins that phase of Moses' mission that probably seemed in some sense quite natural to him, for it was a phase of action. After his fruitless appeal to Pharaoh, it is his task to bring the ten plagues on Egypt.

In fairy tales and myths, when a character brings a curse on another, it usually involves a magic formula. Something must be spoken. "Double, double, toil and trouble," the witches of *Macbeth* ominously proclaim as they stir the caldron. Even in the Bible, at several points characters mouth a curse of some sort. Stories of magical catastrophes usually incorporate a hex or charm. We might expect that the plagues too will be the product of a special formula to be spoken at the appropriate time by Moses.

That would, however, go contrary to Moses' nature, and God knows well that this leader does not yet have faith in the power of words. Moses' attempts at speaking have failed—first when trying to make peace between the fighting Hebrew slaves in his youth, and now with Pharaoh. So we read that God instructs Moses to invoke the plagues *by action*. Moses never utters a formula to begin a plague on Egypt. Instead, he strikes the ground with his staff, holds his staff out over the river, spreads his hands toward the sky, throws dust into the air—a whole range of actions, not words. Learning is a gradual process, and Moses must begin where he is—in the realm of action.

Eventually the accumulation of disasters visited upon Egypt accomplishes its end, and the slaves win their freedom. After the children of Israel are freed from Egypt, after they have marched through the sea and seen their enemies vanquished once and for all, the apex of the biblical tale is recounted in the revelation at Mount Sinai. Sinai is the ultimate reason for liberation. The children of Israel are not only liberated *from* slavery—they are liberated *to* Sinai, to the revelation of God. They have become free to accept and understand a message. At the mountain their mission will become clear.

Moses ascends the peak of Sinai to receive God's word, while the people ring around the bottom of the mountain expectantly. This is the pinnacle of the biblical account. When Moses receives the ten commandments from God, the Hebrew makes a very subtle point about what is occurring. For in the Hebrew, the ten commandments are not called "commandments." In Hebrew they are the ten "sayings," the ten *devarim*. God's critical revelation to the people is not a deed, not a further display of magic and miracle. While it is true that the people have seen the plagues, the splitting of the sea, and various other marvels and wonders, these phenomena are not of the essence. The miracles of liberation were effected in order to bring the children of Israel to the foot of a mountain where God can transmit *words*. All of the supernatural wizardry, the dazzling effects, culminate in speech: the miracle has its ultimate manifestation in the word.

This is the next step in Moses' education. Moses begins to understand that God is, after all, a God of words, of *devarim*. He cannot escape the recognition that when God offers the centerpiece of legislation to the Israelites, it is a granting of *devarim*. The reader recalls what Moses has said about himself, that he is not a man of *devarim*. Now he realizes how important those *devarim* that he forswore are to the God whom he worships.

That God operates through words is already known to the biblical reader. For the world has been made with words. At the outset of the Bible, we read that even creation is a function of language, of speech. The Bible recounts: "God *said*, 'Let there be lights'. . . . And it was so" (Gen. 1:14, 15). God does not spin the world on a finger or wave a wand. At the generative moment in biblical history there is no greater creative act than selecting and speaking the proper word. As one of the morning prayers in the Jewish worship service phrases it: "Blessed be God who spoke and the world came into being." The same God who creates with a word now connects to the children of Israel and to their destiny through *devarim*, through words.

At the very moment that Moses comes into possession of the commandments, the *devarim*, there is a startling story that highlights the tension between words and action in Moses' life. Moses has been on top of Mount Sinai, receiving the Divine word. Now he descends the mountain, holding the tablets of God. It is more than the summit of an individual's life and career: it is the pivot of human history.

Moses descends the mountain carrying the tablets of God in his hands. As he reaches the bottom, he is confronted by a horrible sight: the children of Israel have betrayed him and betrayed God. They are dancing about an idol, a golden calf, that they fashioned in his absence. Moses' own brother Aaron has aided the people in this abomination. The moment of triumph has been reversed, and all is darkness.

Moses' reaction is precisely what we would expect of someone who cannot believe that words, the very words he holds in his own hands at the moment, are as effective a response as action. He smashes the tablets of God upon the ground at the foot of the mountain.

Moses has once again acted in a way reminiscent of his earlier years—rage at injustice leads to violent action.

There are many rabbinic stories and speculations concerning those broken tablets. The moment combines elements of personal tragedy, communal treachery, Divine displeasure; the calf mutely mocks all God's hopes for this stubborn people.

On top of this is a tremendous paradox: by smashing the tablets, a human being, Moses, destroys the eternal word of God. Why did he do it? Some of the commentators argue that it was simply from anger, as the Bible itself declares, that Moses smashed the tablets. Others argue that anger was alloyed with sadness. Still others say it was out of weakness.

Those who argue for weakness develop the talmudic story that after Moses saw the golden calf, he looked up at the tablets and saw that the letters had vanished! Seeing that the tablets were empty he was so discouraged that they grew too heavy for him, slipped from his hand, and broke at the foot of the mountain.

Why did the tablets appear empty? We must recall the context of the story. Moses has just pulled off an astonishing string of triumphs. He has stood up to a tyrant and liberated a people. Although he has taken on the burden

of leadership only reluctantly, its results must have dazzled him. Here is a child born under a sentence of death
negotiating with Pharaoh, saving a nation, defeating
Egypt, leading the people through the wilderness, pro-
ducing vast marvels at the wave of his hand.

In terms of Moses' life alone, in terms of the curve of
his own personal destiny, this moment has an almost unbearable poignancy. Here he is, after all, at the crowning
instant of his life; he is holding the very word of God in
his hands. For one born to an enslaved nation, one loath
to assume the mission entrusted to him, the dizziness of
success must be nearly unbearable.

Yet instead of celebration there is destruction. Violence
supplants joy. Holiness gives way to the horror of a false
god.

The fall from the heights is devastating. He could
humble Pharaoh, but he cannot tame the idolatrous ap-
petites of his own people. This moment is a thorough
betrayal of all Moses has done. No wonder the tablets
suddenly appear empty; the sense of his failure has destroyed his previous success. That awful moment erases
the memory of past achievement. Moses has fought hard,
and now, as he sees the children of Israel dancing and
singing around a calf made of gold, he suddenly views
everything he has accomplished as worthless, empty. He
sees the tablets as blank.

This was among the most powerful lessons Moses
learned about words. For the sin of the golden calf was
not so much that the children of Israel proposed for themselves a new god. Rather, they wanted a substitute for
Moses. As the Bible records: "When the people saw that
Moses was so long in coming down from the mountain,
the people gathered against Aaron and said to him, 'Come,

make us a god who shall go before us, for that man Moses, who brought us from the land of Egypt—we do not know what has happened to him' " (Exod. 32:1). As several traditional commentators point out, what the people desired was not a new invisible, powerful God, but a visible representative of God—a new Moses. Moses was the envoy of the Almighty. Once he was gone, the people panicked.

What the children of Israel could not do, what this band of slaves had not yet learned, was to believe in the invisible. They were trapped by sight. The Israelites had emerged from Egypt, a massive civilization in which they had doubtless learned to respect, even revere, the fabulous monuments, pyramids, artistry—all that one could *see*. In Egypt the visible was elevated to sanctity. Pharaoh, a living presence, a tangible, palpable person, was a god. In Egypt even the realm of the invisible was made visible—the dead were mummified, preserved, kept so that one could still see them, as if sight were eternity and invisibility were oblivion. To this day in Egypt one can see the ancient cities of the dead, where the invisible world of death is made manifest.

Of course, in the Bible, in the Jewish tradition, the opposite conceptions hold. The greatest reality for Judaism is the invisible. God is precisely that which cannot be seen. In the Jewish prayer service, the moment of most fervent devotion is the moment when the worshiper covers his or her eyes. The unseen is Ultimate. In this, triumphantly, God resembles nothing so much as the word—the invisible entity that carries all meaning.

Now Moses' reaction takes on a richer context. He has come to understand more about the realm of the invisible, both God and the word, only to return to a people trapped in the visible. They have built an idol so that they can see something. Moses' hopes are dashed. The patient education of the word cannot cure this people. Suddenly seeing the word as insubstantial, he casts down the tablets.

The story might have ended there, but in this instance destruction is a prelude to renewal. The words cannot be destroyed by splintering the tablets on which they are written. Once spoken, they will not be revoked. The letters are themselves more lasting than the slab of stone on which they were engraved.

Moses fashions a second set of tablets. The Rabbis point out that while God alone wrote the first set of tablets, the tablets Moses smashed, Moses and God together wrote the second. Of the first set, the Bible reads: "When God finished speaking with him on Mount Sinai, He gave Moses the two tablets . . ." (Exod. 31:18). Regarding the second set, God said to Moses, "Carve two tablets of stone like the first, and I will inscribe upon the tablets . . ." (Exod. 34:1). The second was by its nature a set tempered with human wisdom because it was born of human failure. God has enabled Moses to join the process of fashioning the eternal tablets. Moses has begun to learn the power of the word, its limitations, and the glorious truth that even when smashed, it can be renewed.

Moses' experience anticipated the historic truth of the ten commandments. For we no longer have the tablets. The ark that bore them is gone and the actual stone on which they were wrought has long since disappeared. But though the tablets are gone, the words endure.

Having brought the people through this harrowing experience, Moses begins a series of statements, exhortations, and speeches to the children of Israel. Again and again in the biblical account, Moses is called upon to do precisely what he initially fears—he is called upon to speak. He prays, he cajoles, he talks to the people and to God in a string of monologues and dialogues, trying to fulfill his mission. The law that he has delivered to them is a verbal palace, a cavalcade of words. There are thunderous words, words that initiate or emphasize action, but Moses' teaching remains in the realm of rhetoric. At first it appears that Moses has learned to supplant force with fluency. He understood the meaning of God's speech to humanity. Moses now legislates in language. He realizes how critical language is to motivate the actions he desires. He has triumphed.

Yet at a crucial moment, Moses proves incapable of rising to the height of words God demands of him. At one juncture in the people's trek through the desert, they complain for lack of water. Moses, tried beyond endurance, can no longer suffer the constant bickering and complaining of the Israelites. He has suffered and struggled with them; he has worked so hard, and they are so ungrateful. The text reads:

> The people quarreled with Moses, saying, "If only we had perished when our brothers perished. . . . Why did you make us leave Egypt to bring us to this wretched place, a place with no grain or figs or vines or pomegranates? There is not even water to drink!"
>
> Moses and Aaron came away from the congregation to the entrance of the Tent of Meeting, and fell on their faces. The Presence of the Lord appeared to them, and the Lord spoke to Moses saying, "You and your brother Aaron take the rod and

assemble the community, and before their very eyes order the rock to yield its water. . . ."

Moses took the rod from before the Lord, as He had commanded him. Moses and Aaron assembled the congregation in front of the rock; and he said to them, "Listen, you rebels, shall we get water for you out of this rock?" And Moses raised his hand and struck the rock twice with his rod. Out came copious water, and the community and their beasts drank.

But the Lord said to Moses and Aaron, "Because you did not trust Me enough to affirm My sanctity in the sight of the Israelite people, therefore you shall not lead this congregation into the land that I have given them." (Num. 20:3-12)

God instructs Moses to speak to a rock so that it will yield water. But Moses, out of an understandable anger and impatience, strikes the rock rather than speaking to it. Some identify Moses' true sin as hubris—he says, ". . . shall *we* get water for you out of this rock," implying that Aaron and Moses, not God, are responsible for the miracle. Although the explanation is interesting, it is likelier, given Moses' history with words and action, that the root of the trouble is the action that most commentators identify with Moses' sin—striking the rock instead of speaking to it, as he was commanded.

God's punishment is undeniably harsh. For forty years Moses fought to bring the people into the land. Nonetheless, this single episode will end his quest. Now he will be denied the opportunity of entering the land himself. Some interpreters seek to justify the punishment, pointing out that Moses was a leader, and as such, his behavior was very carefully scrutinized by the people. Others argue that it was in fact a favor to Moses, since he was not the appropriate leader for the land, and was better off leaving the people with Joshua. With all the plausible explanations, the punishment still disturbs us. We are left uneasy.

The explanation may go deeper than Moses' being an example. We need only pursue the theme we have traced up to this point. The text itself gives us a subtle clue when the Hebrew employs the word *vayach*: "and he struck." For this is the *same word* used in the Bible when, years before, Moses struck the Egyptian. There it was *vayach et Hamitzri*, "and he struck the Egyptian." Now it is *vayach et haselah*, "and he struck the rock." Despite the years and intervening instruction, Moses has not learned the crucial lesson—that God's instruction must be inculcated not by action alone, but by the appropriate word. The man of deeds has not yet fully appreciated that life and death are not only in the visible miracle, but in the tongue.

We might imagine how frustrating it was for Moses to see his people powerless throughout his youth. They cringed under the lash of the Egyptian master. As slaves, any expression of physical power was forbidden to them. They could never lash out. Understanding the frustration of the powerless, Moses comes to overestimate the value of physical force and the effectiveness of brute power. The danger is that his temperament will be transferred to the people, that they will leap from being a community of slaves to being a community of warriors.

The danger is compounded by the fact that they will soon need to conquer the land. Israel will not be handed to them. Yet if they adopt the demeanor of their former masters, if they come to rely on power and force alone, if their docility turns into savagery, then the society that they create will not survive. God seeks to instruct them in a greater power, one they will require to rule themselves. That is not the power of force, but of reason, of rule, of law, and of language. When their greatest leader, Moses, shows that at critical moments he has recourse only to force, the key to their survival is undermined. Moses is counteracting the essence of God's teaching. Perhaps that is his true sin.

Still, Moses' saga does not end with transgression. Toward the end of the Torah, we see that Moses has learned much, and still has much to teach. He has been punished severely for his transgression. God forbade his entrance into the land of Israel. The goal toward which Moses has worked and strived his whole life is being denied him. The sting of this end is palpable. Moses, who did not want to undertake this mission and who has fought so hard, is now to be deprived of its crowning moment.

This places before the man of action a terrible choice: what shall he do to leave his influence among the people when there are no more actions to be taken, when he will no longer be there to lead them in the land?

Moses meets this challenge in two ways. The first is a delicate and moving act. The leader who early on showed he knew how to act decisively does not disappoint.

The time has come to choose a successor. Moses has come full circle. First he was the reluctant leader. Then he became the great force in the life of the Israelites, taking naturally to his role as molder of the people's morals and character. Now he is about to relinquish the position he has held for so long. It is a difficult moment, one calling for sensitivity. For Moses knows well that if the transfer is not complete and the people do not develop allegiance to his successor, everything he has worked for will be destroyed.

Although God instructs him on how to transfer power, in the end the critical action lies with Moses. By subtly altering God's instruction, Moses achieves a wonderful effect.

The Lord said to Moses, "Ascend these heights of Abarim and view the land that I have given to the Israelite people. When you have seen it, you too shall be gathered to your kin, just as your brother Aaron was. For, in the wilderness of Zin, when the community was contentious, you disobeyed My command to uphold My sanctity in their sight by means of the water." Those are the Waters of Meribath-kadesh, in the wilderness of Zin.

Moses spoke to the Lord, saying, "Let the Lord, Source of the breath of all flesh, appoint someone over the community who shall go out before them and come in before them, and who shall take them out and bring them in, so that the Lord's community may not be like sheep that has no shepherd." And the Lord answered Moses, "Single out Joshua son of Nun, an inspired man, and lay your hand upon him. Have him stand before Eleazar the priest and before the whole community, and commission him in their sight. Invest him with some of your authority, so that the whole Israelite community may obey. . . ."

Moses did as the Lord commanded him. He took Joshua and had him stand before Eleazar the priest and before the whole community. He laid his hands

upon him and commissioned him—as the Lord had
spoken through Moses. (Num. 27:12–20, 22, 23)

What does God request of his servant? That he offer to his
successor, to Joshua, "some" of his authority. We can only
imagine how painful this transfer must have been for Moses. He is the only leader this people has ever known. He
has shaped every living memory of leadership among the
Israelites. He led them out of slavery and shepherded them
through the desert. Now he must publicly shift his leadership to another. The transfer is made doubly painful, for
Moses is deprived of the leader's usual solace in the ancient world: he is not transferring power to his own children. Moses' own sons play no part in the guidance of the
nation. Unlike his brother Aaron, two of whose children
will succeed him, Moses must offer the mantle to one outside his family, to Joshua.

The transfer is not straightforward. Moses does not
precisely follow God's instruction. For God tells him to
"Single out Joshua son of Nun, an inspired man, and lay
your hand upon him." What does Moses do? "He took
Joshua and had him stand before Eleazar the priest and
before the whole community. He laid *his hands* upon him."
Although God requested that Moses use only one hand,
Moses placed both hands on Joshua's head. God, in solic-
itude for Moses' pain, was requiring Moses to transfer
only "some" of his authority to Joshua. But Moses knew
that if Joshua was to meet the challenge of the future he
would need every bit of authority he could muster. While
Moses is being punished for his overzealous devotion to
action, he uses this opportunity to act in a way that highlights his selflessness. Moses will not deprive Joshua or

the people of what they need because of the demands of his own ego. He will lay his hands upon him.

The end approaches for this extraordinary man. The people, and the reader, have followed him through an astonishing journey and a remarkable transformation. Moses is not a superhuman who merely awaited a chance to display his exceptional strength. He does not spring fully grown into leadership. He is more impressive than that—for he has changed, deepened, grown. Against the stark tableau of the wilderness, Moses has developed from a willful young director of a revolution to a hero who changes history, becoming all the while a more faithful and resourceful servant of God.

Facing his own mortality, the end of his own leadership, Moses must decide how his influence can be made to last. His successor has been chosen and he must depart from the people. What should be his final legacy?

No single deed could suffice to encompass the entirety of what Moses wished to teach. Looking out at his people for the last time, it must have seemed to Moses ironic that though he had made such an impression over the years with miracles and battles, with wonders and deeds, now all his action was over. His last campaign had been fought, his last path-clearing strides had been taken. The colossus of Israelite history was about to die, and the man who could not speak needed to find a way to leave a message with a people that, so often in the past, would not listen.

The final book of the Torah, Deuteronomy, is the farewell speech of Moses. His great concern in this book is that the people remember what he has taught. The words "hear" and "listen" are strewn throughout this book.

Moses knows it is his last chance to make an impression. All he can leave behind is his words.

Poignantly, this final book of the Bible, which in English we call Deuteronomy, in Hebrew is called the book of *Devarim*, the book of words. The very man who insisted to God that he was not a man of *devarim*, a man of words, becomes precisely that—the man of *devarim*, the man whose long farewell address enters history as the book of *Devarim*. The transformation is complete, and the message manifest. God took a man who did not understand *devarim*, showed that revelation consisted of *devarim*, and finally reached the point where Moses can begin to embody this Divine lesson—such that Moses has himself become, quite literally, a man of *devarim*. What God requires of Moses is that he learn and understand the power that is involved in being able to speak. Moses' eloquence begins in honesty. He has learned how to wield the power of the word.

The transformation, which has been taking place throughout the Bible, reminds us that God's choice is quite deliberate. Moses has to wrench words from inside himself. He cannot simply summon the phrase that would placate and please. Rather than the gentle comfort of rolling phrases and smooth oratory, God's leader has to prove by his inner struggle that he shares the people's plight. The leader must also have a catch in his throat, not spread ready rhetoric like a salve over all wounds. Moses cannot lead by means of the easy fluency of the demagogue. His is a hard-earned eloquence. His is less the mastery of the word than the heroism of the word.

The education of Moses is a unique legacy. It will prove a mainstay of a people addicted to the word, to writing and teaching. For the exemplar of this faith is an individual who fled from words, struggled with them, and finally bequeathed a sublime legacy of language. Moses' heroism lies both in all that he said and all that, in the end, he could not say. We feel that as he speaks his last words: behind the beauty of his expression is the young man with a speech impediment, struggling and uncertain, knowing that words will never fully express the combination of sadness, pride, and apprehension that lies in his heart.

Before granting his final blessing on the people, Moses pronounces a poem of witness, called in Hebrew *Ha'azinu*. *Ha'azinu* is Moses' final personal testimony. It is the close of his personal drama. More than that, it is a poem whose force lies in the vitality of words whose intent is to use poetic prophecy to change the world.

Ha'azinu begins: "Give ear, O heavens, let me speak; Let the earth hear the words I utter! May my discourse come down as the rain, My speech distill as the dew" (Deut. 32:1, 2).

Moses has learned the lesson of speech so well that he wishes to do more than merely speak to the people. He implores the universe, heaven and earth, to heed his final words. Moses realizes that this testimony is all he can leave behind, that the words will bear an immortality that can never be his in the flesh. So he stands before the people, the people whom he loves, and warns them, encourages them, leaves them his heritage of language.

Right before the concluding blessing to each tribe, Moses leaves them with a further thought: "Take to heart all the words with which I have warned you this day" (Deut. 32:46). With that, Moses approaches the foot of the mountain where he is to die, and offers his final blessing to the people.

Now the transfer of power is complete; the leadership

has been passed on and the last message has been spoken. The strains of Moses' long, rich life are growing fainter, and he is about to be reclaimed by God. He warns the people that the time has arrived when he can no longer lead them; in the biblical idiom, he is no longer able "to come and go." That phrase, which means to guide and manage, is given a lovely traditional interpretation. According to one commentator, Moses quite literally came and went—he walked into the tent of each Israelite to say goodbye, and when he had left the last tent, when he indeed had finished coming and going, he climbed up Mount Nebo to die. As he silently ascended the mountain, surely the people remembered the Moses who could not speak, and they must have wondered what treasures lay still unspoken in his heart.

The final words of God to Moses are spoken as Moses stands upon the Mountain of Nebo. "And the Lord said to him, 'This is the land of which I swore to Abraham, Isaac, and Jacob, "I will assign it to your offspring." I have let you see it with your own eyes, but you shall not cross there'" (Deut. 34:4). This last, painful time, Moses is told that he will not walk in the land he loves. Moses understands that no action can change the decree. He also knows that no words can change it. There is nothing to say, and nothing to do. As he stands on the mountain next to the God whom he has served and loved, Moses has reached a point beyond even the words he so laboriously learned how to speak.

No response from the man of God is recorded. Moses' final cry, as his first cry, is silent.

The poet Yeats once remarked that the great founders of civilization do not write books—they live lives. Socrates,

Buddha, Jesus—none of them, the poet noted, wrote his own book. Each had disciples who wrote about him. Rather than the desiccated and foreign realm of words, great figures make their mark in action, in deed. It was in life itself that civilization's founders created their art.

Of course, Yeats ignored the singular figure who preceded Jesus, Socrates, and the Buddha. The first founder of Western civilization was different. While Moses lived a full life, while his roles as leader and lawgiver were central, curiously, this man who felt so inarticulate, who avoided his mission because he could not speak, is forever associated with a book called by his name. The Torah,* the core of the Hebrew Bible, is called the five books of Moses. Moses' name is linked forever to the immutable teachings of the Jewish tradition. He is remembered as a lawgiver and a leader, but a crucial part of Moses' legacy is as a model for overcoming not Pharaoh, but his own terrors. Ultimately the unique gift of this remarkable figure is not only that he was willing to fight for his people and his God, but that he was willing to speak for them. For the words wrung out of such reticence, with such depth, have echoed down the ages.

In Judaism there is no single ideal life. Jewish children are not taught that they should grow up to be Moses or David, Sarah or Rebecca. Rather there are characteristics of each of these heroes that we should emulate, but there is no one life to which all should aspire. Indeed, in traditional homes when a parent pronounces a blessing over a child on the Sabbath, the parent hopes that the male child

---

*The term "Torah" is sometimes used to refer to the whole Bible, or even the entire corpus of sacred Jewish literature. But in the strictest sense Torah refers, as here, to the Pentateuch: Genesis, Exodus, Leviticus, Numbers, and Deuteronomy.

will be like Ephraim and Menasseh, one renowned for religious learning, and the other for worldly accomplishment and hopes that the female will be like Sarah, Rebecca, Rachel, and Leah, combining the attributes of each of the matriarchs.

Rather than an exclusive model, Judaism instructs us to understand and emulate the *ideals* inscribed in the Torah, in the Talmud, in the great works of the Jewish tradition. In these texts there will be many models, but no model. For the only comprehensive ideal is God. We are to live our lives inspired by Moses' life as we are inspired by others. More important, however, is to live according to Moses' teaching, Moses' words.

The story of Moses's individual struggle suggests that each individual, even those for whom words are halting and difficult, can learn to speak truth. The refuge of faith grants an inner surety that permits us to release words hidden within us and raise them to the light. In the light, much of what seems horrible is endurable and conquerable. Shadows magnify all fears. The words cannot be spoken, however, if we cannot find them buried inside of ourselves. That is a task of personal archaeology, and it requires that we excavate inside. The process is gradual and can be painful. That is why the example of Moses is so potent and to the point. His impediment drove him forward, and out of his stammering came sentences that would ring down the ages.

To learn to speak is difficult and requires a pathway. For those who would seek to learn, the Jewish tradition is such a path, a path of words.

≈

FIVE

Words in Judaism

Take words with you, and return to the Lord.

HOS. 14:3

M oses slowly inched out of the isolation of his self by learning to speak. The solitary shepherd was brought into the community of Israel by God, who insisted that Moses begin to communicate. Through that communication, Moses himself became a model. As Judaism grew, it never lost the lesson that words are central to a religious tradition, to living a full life. As God taught Moses how to speak, Judaism would teach its adherents throughout the generations the same lessons. A great tradition does more than seek to fashion human action. It recognizes that action and words are often inseparable. Each human being lives simultaneously on the planes of motion and stillness, of doing and being, of speaking and silence. Moses' life was a trajectory, beginning in action, continuing in his training and mastery of the word, and ending in silence. Yet throughout his life, all the elements mixed together: Moses never forgot how to act when action was called for, and the power of silence was never far from him. In this we are heirs of his teaching. As each of us needs to learn how to act, we need to learn how to speak. And we must learn what it is to stand silent.

Judaism is a training ground in the importance of words. Part of that training is rooted in the assumptions of Judaism, in its beliefs about the world. Part of it is rooted in the historical experience of the Jewish people.

The infancy of Israel was spent in Egypt, a society shaped by magnificent monuments, by the pyramids and monoliths of a great ancient culture. Egypt left its mark in the landscape, visible testimony to its grandeur. It was a civilization carved in stone.

The Jews who came forth from Egypt did not create a world of monuments. Rejecting the inheritance of their oppressors, they created instead a culture of words. Israel carried not stones but stories into the wilderness and throughout its wanderings. The culture of Israel was conditioned by the lessons of exile and by the renunciation of Egypt. This nation, a unique example of a people born outside their land, was shaped by the stories they told of a home they had never seen.

The Lesson of Homelessness

A man had been wandering in the forest for several days unable to find a way out. Finally he saw another man approaching. He asked him, "Brother, will you please tell me the way out of the forest?" Said the other, "I do not know the way out either,

for I too have been wandering here for many days.
But this much I can tell you. The way that I have
gone is not the way."

So it is with us. We know that the way we have
been going is not the way. Now let us join hands
and look for the way together.

—Rabbi Hayyim of Zans

The Adam and Eve story contains much of the biblical
message in microcosm. This story of origins sets the stage
for all subsequent human history. For the denouement of
the Adam and Eve story teaches a basic dynamic of human
history: the experience of exile, and the intense longing to
return home.

The Torah is dominated by the theme of wandering.
It begins when Adam and Eve leave the garden and continues in the trek through the desert. The garden is the
opposite of the wilderness; one lush and perfect, the other
stark, even brutal. Together these two environments
dominate the biblical landscape, but the wilderness is the
backdrop of four-fifths of the biblical tale, and wandering
is the central event in the Torah. If the garden dominates
as well, it is because the garden is the idyllic spot toward
which human beings will turn again and again in their
dreams. The garden is the ideal whose hazy memory retains its hold on our imaginations and our hearts. The
garden, full of the promise of ripeness and life, is the place
where there is freedom without the attendant agonies of
constant obligation and vigilance.

After Adam and Eve sin, God warns them that they
are being kicked out of Eden forever. The decree marks
the certain end of our brief sojourn. God has decided that
humanity will no more inhabit this preserve of paradise.

Adam and Eve have forfeited their rights; for the rest of time, there will be no more citizens of Utopia.

God blocks the way to paradise. No mortal is agile enough to slip by the guardians of the garden. Notice what God does not do—*God does not destroy paradise*. The obvious solution, if God desires that humanity remain permanently outside the garden, would be to rid the world of Eden forever. Then humanity would be resigned to the certainty of eternal toil, to sweat and pain and irredeemable hardship. But God chooses to station sentries on the road to the garden, to protect it with angels and a fiery sword. Anyone who has read the Bible up to this point, or knows anything about human nature, realizes that human beings will expend endless ingenuity and effort to overcome any obstacle to paradise. As long as the garden exists, we will try to climb back inside its portals. God did not crush the dream, because had there been no paradise to return to, all the struggle and the wandering would have been pointless. The perfect place must be out of the reach of reality but within the grasp of imagination. Childhood must be distant but remembered. Hope must be dimmed, but never extinguished. Paradise can never be seen, but we can speak about it, we can tell the story, we can conjure Eden in imagination, in our words.

The initial exile leaves human beings without a home, but with the resources to recreate home, if only in our minds. The rest of the Bible points up the resources that are bequeathed to us by God, even as home is snatched away: the ability to understand the difference between what is and what was and to spin fantasies of what might be and to communicate them in words. The beginning of wandering contains the seeds of hope. The garden still beckons, hidden from view but abiding, unknown but imagined.

But expulsion is not the end of the human journey in the Torah. The most surprising result is yet to come. For this most influential book in history does not have an ending. The Pentateuch, the foundation stone of the Bible, is a fragment. This most carefully crafted work, in which each word counts, each nuance is plotted and planned, never finishes its tale.

The entire Torah points toward a promised land. The first book, Genesis, is a family drama, the initial shaping of a clan who descends, for reasons of famine and family, into Egypt. After hundreds of years of slavery, there is a giant pageant of miracles, of plagues and the split sea, of promise and liberation. The children of Israel are freed to wander in the desert on the way to the Promised Land.

On each step of the journey, through myriad difficulties, the people envisage a splendid ending. The hope of salvation dangles before their eyes. They will march triumphant into God's good land.

Coming into Canaan, soon to be Israel, is not a mere epilogue to the tale. It is not a glorious by-product of the real focus of liberation and triumph. *Arrival in the Promised Land is the whole point.* In the four books that describe the Israelites' wanderings—Exodus, Leviticus, Numbers, and Deuteronomy—there is no doubt that liberation entails the ushering in of a new age on the land. Entry to the land of Israel is not an incidental end, but the inevitable climax. Leaving Egypt is meaningless without arrival in Israel. No one wishes to be liberated merely to wander in the wasteland. Security, even in enslavement, is to be preferred over endless wandering. That is why the Israelites repeatedly complain, when confronted by hunger or by enemies, that Moses has plucked them from the land of Egypt. As terrible as Egypt was, it seems preferable to the inhospitable emptiness of the desert. Moses keeps them on track by assuring them that the desert is not a postscript, but a prelude. Painting word pictures of the paradise to come, Moses maintains his hold on the people.

The Israelites were lured from Egypt by visions of Eden. Israel will be a land of milk and honey, of promised perfection. Israel was, in some sense, the great symbolic return anticipated from the time that Adam and Eve were ushered out of Eden.

Remarkably, however, when the Torah ends, when the last pages and the final verses of Deuteronomy are read, the Israelites are not in the land. They stand at the edge of the Promised Land, but have not entered. We are left, after this amazing journey, in the wilderness.

Later on, in the book of Joshua, the Israelites do enter Canaan and conquer it. But the book of Joshua was not made part of the Torah itself, of the five books. It was given no place in the revered scroll that stands in the ark of every synagogue and that is read on a regular basis in prayer services. It is far less significant. The triumphal moment of the Israelite people, the presumed climax of the story, becomes a sideshow.

Each year, the Torah is read in a repeating cycle. One portion is designated to be read each week until the five books are completed. The cycle ends with the Israelites prepared to enter the land, and just when arrival seems imminent, we are snatched back, we start again with the creation of the world, at the beginning of Genesis. It is an eternal succession of expectation and frustration. Why?

One message clearly conveyed by the text is that there

is no perfect Promised Land, except as a promise. Daily life, as it is lived, is the wilderness. There is suffering and pain. There is need and scarcity; the world is parched and fallow. For all the blessings that we share, only the most callous could believe that in this world we are in the Promised Land.

What the Torah teaches by ending in the desert is the critical lesson of all subsequent human history: that we are unredeemed, that the Promised Land is unattained and, for the meanwhile, even unattainable.

The wilderness is not only an external condition, however. There is another prior wilderness, the inner landscape, which the Israelites must confront. In the desert they faced themselves, their own fear and hesitance. Moses warns them at the end of the Torah that when they enter Israel, they will still be the same erring people who have wandered through the desert. The scenery may change, but the soul carries within both the seeds of the garden and the sands of the wilderness.

The wilderness is not only an image of human unhappiness, it is the symbol for inner struggle. As the Rabbis state, understanding the deepest symbolism of wilderness: "One who does not make himself open to all like a wilderness cannot acquire wisdom and Torah." All human beings travel in the wilderness, all need the insecurity the wilderness embodies.

The Torah cannot end because it reflects the human condition, which does not end. The struggle is eternal. In the Torah it is fought on the terrain of words—the stories told, the laws pronounced, all the exhortations offered the fledgling nation.

Some words will be repeated again and again; they will become part of the people's self-understanding. For the words of the desert are the words inside. They are words of barrenness and of birth, of struggle, of long distances without clear destinations.

In the Bible, the Israelites ceaselessly complain, moan, cry. They bewail the lack of food and the threats from enemies. There is civil insurrection. In place of the passive and grateful band of freed slaves we might expect, there is a quarrelsome group that is seized by fear. While God has promised them a glorious future, they cannot eat promises or drink visions. They are alone and afraid in a vast wilderness.

That is why they are given the Torah. The Torah was given in the desert because one does not need a Torah in paradise. The Torah is not a map of the promised land, it is a guide through the wilderness. And the wilderness is life as lived in a world that is still far from perfect. The Torah, through its stories, its history, its prescriptions, will serve throughout the generations as a means of coping with the wilderness, the terrain in which we all live.

So the Israelites learned that wilderness and wandering are not just a geographical condition. They are the very stuff of life. To create a human culture that matters and that lasts is to create a culture that will accommodate the wilderness. A wilderness cannot be tamed with monuments or monoliths. Shifting sands cover palaces as they do footprints. The desert wind howls away any pretense to permanence. What can be carried and preserved through the desert is the message. What we retain from those years of wandering are the stories, the ordinances, the inspiration. The wilderness is made bearable by words.

When Judaism peers back into its history to the generation of the desert, what emerges is a people who snatched from that difficult time the word of God. God's faithfulness is the security given to the Israelites as they made their way through the barrenness. As it says in Jeremiah: "O generation, behold the word of the Lord! Have I been like a desert to Israel, or like a land of deep gloom?" (2:31). Though the people wandered in gloom, the word of God was the antidote to emptiness. Beholding it, they understood how they were preserved by the word.

The tale of the Torah presaged later Jewish history, and its words underlie the eternality of the wandering. Searching for home did not end with the conquest of the land; the fears did not die in the desert. For even reaching the land was but a temporary haven. Beginning with the first exile into Babylonia some seven hundred years later, and on into the modern age, a large part of the Jewish people has ever been homeless. Jews have traveled throughout the world, unable to find a fixed place to settle. In a poignant custom, traditional Jewish homes left a corner of the house unpainted to indicate that this dwelling was temporary, a stop on the way to home. Sometimes moving from place to place was voluntary, more often it was not. Impermanence burned itself deep into the Jewish consciousness. To exist was to be displaced. The Torah foretold the fate of its adherents. The desert was an image destined to recur throughout Jewish history.

The theme of exile preoccupied Jews, wending its way into liturgy, literature, everyday customs, and ceremonies. An additional day was added to certain holidays for those residing outside of Israel. The Passover meal ended with the hopeful declaration "Next Year in Jerusalem." Jews who were vintners or farmers all over the world prayed for rain not when their crops needed rain, but when the hills of Jerusalem required rain. They implored God to send dew not when their own fields were needy, but when the fields of Israel were dry. The cycles of the year, the prayers and holidays, were observed according to the climate and calendar of Israel. In the apt image of Rabbi Henry Fisher, Jews were like travelers who kept their watches set on the time at home, so as to keep in mind the "real" time. Jews kept their spiritual clocks set to the time at home, the rhythms of life in Israel, which served both to fortify their souls and to reinforce their sense of dislocation.

Given such an orientation and such a sense of constant displacement, Jews did not create the soaring or solid monuments of other cultures. They could not forget that their dwelling was temporary. What Jews sought to create was a portable culture, one that fit both the theology of Judaism and its history. We sought a culture of meanings, not of monuments.

Words could be carried from land to land and from place to place. Inside the head of a Jew, worlds of messages could exist. Songs, stories, parables, and prayers formed the lasting culture, which was, paradoxically, the invisible culture. Shrines do not survive. Only what you could not see lasted.

"Not marble nor the gilded monuments / Of Princes shall outlive this pow'rful rhyme," wrote Shakespeare in his fifty-fifth sonnet. Some fifteen hundred years before, the Psalmist had written, "The idols of the nations are silver and gold. . . . Those who fashion them . . . shall become like them. . . . [But] O Lord, Your name endures forever" (Ps. 135:15, 18, 13). The name of God, the word, will outlive the silver, the gold, the gilded monuments. In his idiom, the bard echoes the certainty of the religious singer—even the most precious substance crumbles before the Name, before the word.

Speaking: The First Model

God trained Moses to speak. That model would pervade the Jewish tradition. One of the reasons God chose Moses may be precisely that he maintained his perspective on the visual splendor of Egypt. God wished to wean Israel from the ancient Egyptian understanding of the world. To see beneath the structures of stone to the spiritual realities of the society, to understand the oppression hidden beneath the opulence—that was the task of a leader.

Moses grew up in the palace of Pharaoh. He was raised on the luxuries of the royal life-style. When Moses is grown, and goes out into society, one would expect him to be a part of the brilliant culture that flourished all about him. A social conscience was not the primary legacy of an education in Pharaoh's palace. Yet in the midst of this grandeur, Moses sees not beauty, but anguish. The Bible reads: "Some time after that, when Moses had grown up, he went out to his kinsfolk and witnessed their suffering" (Exod. 2:11). On his first recorded foray into the world, Moses sees not the magnificence of Egypt, but its underside of cruelty and deprivation. Moses sees the society through the eyes not of a worshiper of wealth, but of one who is fit to become a prophet. It is an attitude he bequeathed to his descendants. Thus the Talmud says that eventually the nations of the world will be judged for their designs and purposes. And they will be condemned if they built bridges merely to collect tolls, marketplaces simply to accumulate wealth; if they created armies not for defense, but for wars of pillage and spoliation. Accomplishment without aims is empty. Structure without sanctity is vain.

With Moses, Judaism began a great experiment to build a culture along a different model, a model whose central bearer of meaning was not the object, not what one could touch and see, but the ephemeral, invisible word.

Words of Creation and Faith

Judaism has no sacred ritual objects. If a Jew drops any ritual object, a candlestick, a spice box, a wine cup, it is simply retrieved. But when one drops a sacred book, it must be kissed. The name of God contained in the book is holy. The word carries the flame of sanctity as does nothing else save life itself.

That is why a sage of the Jewish tradition is a sort of living book. Sacred books of Judaism, which may not be destroyed, are buried (in the Hebrew, *ganuz*, literally "hidden") when they are no longer usable. So the Talmud says, praising the sage Rabbi Eliezer the Great upon his burial, "A scroll of Law was hidden." Centuries before, as the Israelites brought the coffin of Joseph out of Egypt and carried it with them across the desert, they bore it next to the ark carrying the tablets of God's law. The Talmud explains that when someone would ask about the curious conjunction of the two boxes side by side, the people would respond, "He who lies in this ark fulfilled all that lies in that one." One could not hope for a more honorable epitaph.

The central religious objects in Judaism are scrolls, books, commentaries; the central quest in Judaism is the attempt to bring the sacred into language, to make the ineffable expressible.

There seems one great contradiction to this idea—

the Western Wall of the Temple, which is today a venerated object. The Western Wall in Jerusalem is a series of stone blocks weathered by time. It is the outer wall of the second Temple, destroyed in the year 70 C.E. When the Temple itself stood, however, what was its holiest spot? The central room, the Holy of Holies, which contained the tablets of God's law. The Temple was sacred *not* because of the external structure, but because of the words that dwelt within. The holiest moment of the year was when the High Priest would enter the central sanctuary of the Temple *and pronounce the name of God*. Sanctity was embodied in speech.

So today, when Jews piously gather around the wall, they are paying homage to the remnant of the structure that once housed words of God. Stones are mute blocks of remembrance. What eloquence is found in those craggy blocks is lent by the memory of the sacred message the Temple represents, an emblem of the days before the brutality of history left us with just this fragment.

The first-time visitor to the wall cannot help but think this spot seems an improbable place for pilgrimage. The wall boasts none of the grandeur, none of the artistry, that characterizes so many of the world's great religious monuments. In a city drenched in antiquity, the wall is one more ancient site.

Yet the mute stones tell an interesting story in our own day as well. For although the tablets are gone now, the deepest wish of the worshiper is that the stones should somehow speak. A visitor to this remnant of the destroyed Temple sees a strange sight. Inside the cracks between the stones are notes, thousands of them, wedged in the crevices. Each note contains a prayer, a few words, an extended plea—supplications held in place by the massive stones. The stones do not speak, but between their ancient contours they clutch diverse hopes of the human heart. Whether words offered at one place lift higher than at another place none can say with certainty. But the wall represents the ultimate aim of Jewish prayer, which is to turn even the inanimate into prayerful objects. Not only people, but all things should pray, should praise. Even stones must speak, and if there are no longer tablets to embody God's word at the center of the Temple, then the private pious wishes of worshipers will speak on behalf of what was lost. The cries cannot be heard, but they lose none of their eloquence for their stillness. The wall is turned into a fortress of words.

This does not negate the love and attachment Judaism has always felt toward the physical land of Israel. Return was ever part of Jewish hopes and prayers. People cannot grow fruit with scrolls or cultivate patches of words. But what kept the Jewish people alive, dreaming of the distant land of Israel, of reclaiming their heritage, was the eloquence of the prophets, the evocations of the sages, the teachings of tradition. Notes in the Western Wall represent the conjoining of aspiration and actuality, the word and the world.

Beginning with the Bible, and then the Talmud, Judaism is a spiral of verbal invention, of interpretation, imprecation, give and take, question and response. A modern reader opening a page of the Talmud finds a pageant of language. The wisdom of antiquity jostles against insights of later ages: the Bible is distilled in a second-century law code (the Mishna) followed by a fifth-century commentary (the Gemara) surrounded by the comments of Rashi, an eleventh-century exegete, and the tosafists, thirteenth-century commentators, as well as glosses by scholars from the sixteenth and seventeenth centuries. All of this dialogue across the centuries is a goad to other digests, discussions, and conclusions drawn by scholars up to our own day. The result is a thicket of text quite deliberately designed to be endless—the Talmud begins on page two, informing the eager reader that there is no true beginning or end to the journey of language, of study, of speaking sacred words.

Writing about such a tradition lends itself to a similar style. Books about Judaism tend to be thick with quotations, stories, allusions to other works. Constant cross-reference is a traditional Jewish mode of speaking and teaching. The Rabbis go so far as to state, "One who quotes another by name brings redemption into the world." The world itself is preserved by the perpetuation of teaching and of memory. "Remember the days of old, consider the years of generations past; ask your father, he will inform you. Your elders, they will tell you" (Deut. 32:7). The fabric of tradition is continuous. Each generation draws its patterns, adds a stitch, a seam, adjusts the garment to the climate in which it lives.

This pattern mimics how we begin to speak as individuals as well. A child imitates the sounds, and finally the words, it hears from its parents. In time, the child will begin to evolve his or her own combination of sounds and sense, adding to the stock of meanings in the world. Learning begins in imitation and grows to originality.

We should recall that throughout the Bible the people of Israel are called "the children of Israel." They are being taught slowly, carefully, as one teaches a child. The story of the desert is in part the story of a people who must be guided to the first hesitant sounds of freedom so they might then speak on their own. Yet the words they have been taught in infancy do not leave them. Their own words will not be forgotten. All of it, from the first faltering sounds in the desert to the eloquence of the prophets and sages, is part of an unending struggle to untangle meanings and celebrate joys.

In Judaism, one who writes and does not borrow upon the wisdom of the past, who does not quote the sages or reframe their insights, one who wishes to create meanings without referring to all the meanings that have gone before is one trying to build without first laying the foundation. Or to change the metaphor, as Rava puts it in the Talmud, "A fitting quotation is like bread to the famished."

Still it is strange that, as much as words are added to the tradition in each generation, a vast volume of words are repeated again and again. Studying a page of the Talmud, the same conclusions, insights, mistakes, and triumphs of reasoning are repeated. Prayers that have been uttered millions of times are unchanged in each morning's recitation. Although certain prayers take on a heightened poignancy at one time or another, on the whole the prayers, the debates, the identical words are never exhausted. Unlike the texts of so many civilizations whose ideas have run their course, the dead letters of a moribund world, the words of Judaism remain vital.

That reality has led the Jewish tradition to understand that these words are not inanimate. They do not simply lie on the page to be picked up by the interested reader.

There is something preternaturally alive about the words of Judaism. They shimmer, move, sparkle. They are not merely ink. They are fire.

The Scroll of Fire

"The voice of the Lord kindles flames of fire," writes the Psalmist (Ps. 29:7). God's world is made brilliant, set ablaze without destruction, by God's word. The equation of God's fire and the power of words goes deep through the Jewish tradition. We recall that God first spoke to Moses out of the fire of the burning bush. The great medieval Jewish mystic Abraham Abulafia taught that "the voice of the living God speaks from within the fire, and it dwells within the heart, and thus is speech there." True speech comes from the heart, for that is where the fire of God flares brightest. "From the heavens He let you hear His voice to instruct you; on earth He let you see His great fire; and from amidst that fire you heard His words" (Deut. 4:36).

The mystics teach that the entire Torah is one long name of God. The word of the Torah, they teach, existed as fire in heaven previous to creation. Part of this beautiful mystical idea is based on a reality long past. In ancient times, scrolls were written from beginning to end in unbroken progression, without punctuation, without breaks between words. The reader had to decide where one word ended and another began. So one can envision a scroll as one long continuous word. The deeper implication of this idea is that holiness is unitary, that it is a continuous scroll, stretching eternally, a word that cannot quite be spoken.

~

Why on fire? When God led Israel through the desert, the Bible describes God's Presence as like a column of fire by day. Fire is illumination, brilliance, mystery. In the Bible it is a symbol not of destruction, but of great forces—the stars, the vault of the heavens—magically snatched and brought to earth. The Midrash tells us that fire was a gift to humanity. God told Adam to take two stones and rub them together to create fire. The two stones, in the legend, were called Darkness and the Shadow of Death. In other words, fire, as the God who created it, is what brightens the darkness, what overcomes the terror of death, what brings the illumination of the cosmos down to this mortal arena. Given the proper teaching, one can take even darkness and death and turn them to light. The teaching emerges from the fire that is the letters of the Torah.

According to mystic tradition, the word spelled out in fire in the Torah was the name of God. If we could read the Torah in one breath, pronouncing everything in it, we would be capturing God's name. Of course we cannot read it that way, but it says something important about what speech really is. A word is really the Divine on fire.

Suddenly the prospect of dredging up the hidden words inside us takes on a new dimension. We are learning to unleash and to release the fire inside. We are joining our flame, which is the spark of language, to the primordial fire. The careful reader of the Bible notices that during creation, before the sun is fashioned on the fourth day, there is light: When God says "Let there be lights," there is as yet no sun, no physical means of generating radiance. That is the light, say the mystics, of the Source of all light, the light which emanates from the hidden presence of the Divine. That light is channeled to humanity through the ever-glowing ember of God's word.

Speaking to God

The Jewish tradition maintains that the Torah is a message from God to humanity. But if all that mattered was heeding God's word, we could have been created with ears and without mouths—made only to listen.

From the first, however, we have struggled with speech. Part of that struggle is to find a way to speak to God. What words can advance our cause, or express our yearnings, before the Creator of the Universe?

In a previous chapter we cited the meditation that opens the *Amidah* prayer: "O Lord, open my lips that my mouth may sing your praise." At first glance, that line is peculiar. After all, the words are written in the prayer book. There seems no reason to request God's help. Simple recitation will do.

Of course, the prayer is not a plea for automatic recitation. It touches upon something deeper, a recognition that threads through all the tales in this book.

Authentic speech is not the pronunciation of words. Authentic speech is expressing truth and passion through words. That is why, so often, the deepest speech requires few words. The transmission of information requires accurate speech, not authentic speech. If you wish the salt, you need only enunciate the proper words. But tell someone else of your love, and the words alone will not carry that message through the distance that separates you. The only thing that can bridge the distance is authentic speech, speech that comes from somewhere deeper inside ourselves. We need to ask God to help because we do not wish merely to pronounce the words that are before us. That is a mechanical skill and can be done as fluently by a dictaphone as by a human being. Only a person can pour out his or her heart. "We use words as tools," wrote Abraham Joshua Heschel. "We forget that words are a repository of the spirit."

"Open my lips" in the *Amidak* prayer really means "open my heart." The prayer uses the word "lips" instead of "heart" because it recognizes the intimate connection of speech and emotion, between lips and heart. But unlike human beings, God can read the heart. So why do we need still to speak the words? Why can we not pray as one Rabbi, feeling overwhelmed by the sorrows of the world, is reported to have prayed: "Dear God, I cannot speak all the sorrows in my heart. So I open my heart to you, and I ask you to read all the anguish written thereon."

We pray in words because to speak one's own sorrows is to learn them. What we are asking God for, when we pray that our lips might be opened, is the ability to know our own hearts, to strip away the wall that separates us from ourselves. The prophet promised that one day God would take away our heart of stone and replace it with a heart of flesh. We seek to do that for ourselves when we lift our voices in sincere prayer, which is never free of both gratitude and anger, anguish and anticipation. The prayer is a way of saying to God: "You see that we seek to know ourselves. Help us know ourselves through prayer to You." A prayer is a plumbline dropped down to the center of the soul, a line to disclose our own depths.

Prayers Silent and Spoken

Seeking to say all that we can, we endeavor to go deeper than that which can be spoken. In some peculiar way, prayer is always moving toward, but never quite arriving at, silence. Even the "silent meditation" in the Jewish prayer service, the *Amidah* with which we have been dealing up to this point, is really supposed to be audibly, although softly, spoken. The worshiper must hear his or her own words. To speak words in the recesses of the heart is not the same as to hear them spoken. Words buried inside do not have the force of words that have been heard, even if they have been heard only by the ears of the speaker. To think "I love you" or to think "I am alone" does not wrack the body quite the way that the words—recklessly tossed into the world, or painfully brought forth one by one—can make us shiver with the startling sound of our own truth. "Prayer," wrote Heschel, "lives in words."

In the Talmud, Rava teaches that "words in the heart are not words"—that something must be spoken to be real. The context for this remark is a legal discussion, but much of what we have seen in the Jewish tradition clothes that legal remark in religious garb. Something must be spoken, meanings must be spun out of the emptiness, and that lesson lies behind one of the most beloved of Jewish parables.

The story is told in many forms. One version concerns the great Chasidic master Levi-Yitzhak of Bereditchev. Once, on Rosh Hashana, the Jewish New Year, he saw that the blasts of the shofar, the ram's horn that is sounded as the culmination of the prayer, were not ascending to heaven. Knowing that there must be a blocked or afflicted soul among his congregants, the Rabbi began to look around the congregation.

At the back of the synagogue stood a young shepherd boy. He looked troubled. The Rabbi approached and asked him what was wrong, and the boy explained that he was an orphan and had never learned how to pray. All he had learned was the *aleph-bet*, the Hebrew letters. The Rabbi told him merely to recite the *aleph-bet*, and God would arrange the words. The boy began to chant the letters over and over again. The synagogue began to shake, and Reb Levi-Yitzhak saw the prayers not only of the shepherd but of the whole congregation soaring up to the heavens together with the blasts of the shofar.

Recently, Rabbi Shlomo Riskin told of a beautiful addendum to this story. In the Ukrainian city of Lvov, a certain Chasid was officiating at High Holiday services, and knowing that many of his congregants had been deprived of a Jewish education by the Soviet government, he told them the story of Reb Levi-Yitzhak and the shepherd.

When he reached the end of the story and spoke of how the letters had ascended to heaven, a woman screamed out to the Rabbi: "But we don't know the *aleph-bet*." Deprived of any religious education, they had never even learned to recite the letters of the Hebrew alphabet.

Placing his tallit, his prayer shawl, over his head, and closing his eyes, the Rabbi said: "I will teach them to you." And so he called out "Aleph," the first letter, and the whole congregation responded, crying out "Aleph!" With each letter, the response grew greater. By the time he reached the end of the alphabet, 2,500 voices, voices that had never pronounced a Jewish prayer, were calling out each Hebrew letter, one by one.

~

The beauty of this story lies not only in the sublimity of the moment, but in the assumption behind it. The Rabbi could simply have told the congregation to pray what was in their hearts. He could have asked them to offer up silently to God any hopes and aspirations that moved them. But he knew that the tradition, as in the story of the shepherd, wants inchoate hopes to be spun into sounds, letters, words. We may well imagine that there was more yearning in the simple recitation of the alphabet than in many of the carefully crafted prayers of the learned.

The first lesson of prayer to God is that prayer must find its way to words. For paradoxically, only in speaking words do we discover what is beneath them. Words are the keys to unlatch locks that guard alcoves of the heart, hidden preserves that can be entered and touched only with the aid of speech. Having tapped the well within us, we then advance past words. By reciting all we can, we hope to reach past the domain of words. We hope to come to the moment when all language is exhausted, and the night hangs heavy and meanings we did not know were inside us make their way to God. "There are seventy ways of reciting the Torah," said the Tzartkover Rabbi, "and one of them is through silence."

The Listening God

Our silence and our speech matter because God listens. In the Psalms, those poetic pleas carved from the heart, the Psalmist repeatedly asks God to listen: "Hear my cry, O God" (61:2); "In my distress I called to the Lord" (120:1). Most pointedly, there is Psalm 19 (verse 4): "There is no speech and there are no words whose sound goes un-heard." No word ever uttered has gone unheeded.

This is a central affirmation in Judaism: "I am heard." Some of the most desolate images imaginable are those in which an individual wails with none to hear. That is part of the pain of Shakespeare's King Lear standing on the heath, the rains raging about him as he cries out. For all Lear's agonized eloquence, the wind blows back his words, and each gust drowns out and mocks his cries. In a world without God, the truth and depth of what we say are no guarantee that it will be heard. The most fervent, full-throated cry can be carried off by the wind.

God's attention preserves the eternity of the word. In language, only that which is heard, which can somehow be recorded or preserved, can remain. This is the peculiarity of language, that speaking is not enough; air is the voice's medium, and there must be something, a pen, a human ear, a Divine utterance, to catch the vibrations. "Gather the people to Me," says God, "that I may let them hear My words" (Deut. 4:10). God's words, too, need to be heard. A statue will outlive its creator, and others can come along and see it. But a word spoken, if it is not heard, is forever lost. So it is that some of the most glorious sounds in history have doubtless been lost. There was no one to hear.

Not so in the Jewish tradition, not so for the Psalmist. No sound is lost, no utterance unheard. The ephemeral word outlasts the stone. God's gift is to attend to the pleas of human beings, to what Wordsworth called "the still, sad music of humanity." Judaism hearteningly affirms that God hears when all is still and sad. God hears as well when our music is joyous, triumphant; when it is vicious, and when it is tender. No chord is lost. As the Psalmist writes (139:4) "There is not a word on my tongue but that You, O Lord, know it well."

Listening is not the same as response. Often the assurance that God hears is but a beginning. What we wish for is that God would not only hear, but grant our petition. This, too, troubled the Psalmist, and the Psalms are filled with petitions born of anger and disappointment. "Why, O God, do You forever reject us? Why do you seethe in anger at Your flock?" (74:1). Even this dejected petition is fueled by the belief that God hears. For a moment, when we stub our toes, we may rant at the chair. But only lunatics spend their time screaming at stones or lecturing furniture. Yet we have a sense, an ineradicable sense, that we ought to be able simply to speak out, to scream at the sky. Sometimes in defiance of all we can see, a certainty creeps over us that something must be listening. So we not only praise and hope, we vilify, we agonize, we question. And we wonder—is that vague sense that something is listening, a sense we do not get from objects in the world, is it perhaps God's subtle way of urging us to speak?

Sounds of Prayer

There are moments in the Jewish prayer service when the congregation falls almost silent. The silence is not complete. Even the intimate meditations of the prayer book are formed in words. A silent meditation is really a mumbled meditation, a whispered thought.

This practice underscores a truth about the nature of speech and language in general, and in the Jewish tradition in particular. *In order for your words to be meaningful, you must be able to hear them yourself.* Prayer is addressed to yourself, not just to God. The purpose of prayer is to teach what matters in this world, to fill up an empty heart, to guide, to aid. Part of prayer is a spur to our own conscience and action. The theologian Rabbi Harold Schulweis once remarked, "If you ask me—is prayer heard? I'll ask you— are you listening?" Prayer is directed inward as well as outward, and if we wish our prayers to matter, they must matter to us. To borrow a talmudic phrase, we must permit our ears to hear what our mouths are saying.

The challenge of prayer is to overcome the difficulty of understanding the import of one's own words. For that reason prayers are usually offered in a group. You may not understand what you say. There can be blocks between one's mouth and one's ears. But hearing those same words from the person next to you may suddenly crystallize their meaning. They leap like a spark from one person, from one mouth, to the other. The din that arises from listening to worshipers praying alone together sounds aimless. But something is being passed along. Each person's prayer is reinforced. Each confession is shared. An individual worshiper is in the swaying embrace of the entire community.

Group prayer is important for other reasons as well, but we cannot underestimate the meaning that praying together grants each word: it becomes part of a dialogue. Prayer is not a monologue. It speaks to God and to the community. In the last analysis, religion is not what goes on inside a soul. It is what goes on in the world, between people, between us and God. To trap faith in a monologue, and pretend that it resides solely inside the self, undermines the true interchange of all belief. It allows the egotism of the self to swallow the variety, complexity, and beauty of true dialogue. It is a betrayal of the word.

Kol Nidre

At the holiest moment of the Jewish year is a strange service. Called the Kol Nidre service, it inaugurates the most awesome day on the Jewish calendar, Yom Kippur, the day of atonement. The beginning of such a holiday should correspond to its loftiness. At the outset of that day, one would expect wrenching themes of repentance to carry the worshiper along. As night falls and the holiday begins, a hush takes over the congregation, and a beautiful melody, a haunting minor-keyed masterpiece, is chanted by a Cantor, a representative of the congregation.

Instead of chanting about sin, about the terrible wrongs that human beings do to one another, however, the Cantor chants about vows. All vows, obligations, promises, reads the prayer, that we have made to God and were not able to fulfill, may they all be counted as nothing. May they be erased. In the most prevalent version of the prayer, we pray not that the vows of the past year be annulled, but that the vows we will make in the following year, the vows of the future, be made invalid. It is a curious choice of prayer at the most solemn moment of the year.

Judaism is a tradition that takes the concept of repentance very seriously. Yom Kippur concentrates on sins we have committed in the past, which demand reparation and atonement. It is therefore peculiar indeed to choose this sacred moment to speak about vows and promises. Were the prayer a lilting evocation of evil deeds and consequent sorrow, were we praying that God forget and forgive all the wrongs we have done, it would seem in perfect harmony with the tenor of the day. For Yom Kippur is devoted primarily to wrongs done other people. But we begin with this yearning to erase promises that we have not yet made, promises not between people (which can be canceled only by the parties involved), but between the individual and God.

The meaning of this ritual becomes clear in light of all we have learned so far. Words are never mere words. A promise is not an insubstantial matter. Words spoken to God are real. They entwine the soul of the speaker. When we promise and do not fulfill, we understand that the intentions, and their form, the words, are still stuck to our souls. We need release because words bind. The Midrash teaches in a number of places that for God to speak a word is equivalent to God's performing an action. With the Divine, the word and the action are somehow the same. Although we aspire to that level, although we wish to reach the point where what we say and what we do reach a perfect consonance, we are far from such a height. It remains important that we remember the distance. In that way we will lament that our intentions outstrip our self-knowledge, and that our vows promise what we do not fulfill.

This realization leads us to an interpretation of one of the most enigmatic sayings in literature. When God and Moses first speak with one another, at the burning bush, Moses asks to be told God's name: "Moses said to God, 'When I come to the Israelites and say to them "The God of your fathers has sent me to you," and they ask me, "What is His name?" what shall I say to them?' " (Exod. 3:13).

Moses is apparently interested in some designation that

he can bring back with him, some title that will convince a numbed people. But though God gives a name, we find that Moses never repeats it to the people. The name stays with him. Apparently Moses is really asking for himself. At the moment of consecration to the task of leadership, Moses needs to understand something of the nature of this God who calls upon him to undertake such a monumental mission. God's answer, however, seems to confuse more than it clarifies:

"And God said to Moses, 'I Am that I Am'" (Exod. 3:14).

The answer is puzzling enough in English. But there is a peculiarity to biblical Hebrew that renders it even more confusing. For biblical Hebrew has no present tense. The present is denoted by using the future tense. So "I Am that I Am" can also mean "I will be as I will be." As often happens, however, as the confusion deepens one uncovers the seeds of solution.

A critical lesson to be gleaned from this enigmatic answer is that God is fully realized. Whatever God is, God will continue to be. God's word is as a deed, because there is no disharmony between God's nature now and in the future. As the prophet Isaiah puts it in a beautiful simile: "For as the rain or snow drops from heaven and returns not there, but soaks the earth and makes it bring forth vegetation, yielding seed for sowing and bread for eating, so is the word that issues from My mouth: It does not come back to Me unfulfilled, but performs what I purpose, achieves what I sent it to do" (Isa. 55:10, 11).

Moses needs to understand that the words God speaks are not a vague assurance but a certain promise. He can take on the task of leadership knowing that God will be with him throughout the vagaries and difficulties of his leadership. We, as human beings, need to annul vows because we know that we will err, speak hastily, change our minds, overestimate our capacities, promise from fear, from hope. None of these contingencies apply to God. What God is, God will be.

When we chant the Kol Nidre prayer on Yom Kippur, we are confessing, first and foremost, our distance from the Divine. Our shortcomings are manifest. We change. We vacillate. We cannot always trust our words. Having established that, we proceed to the even more difficult task of examining our deeds.

The remainder of the Yom Kippur service is a masterful interplay of words human and Divine. We quote biblical texts that exhort us to forgive and promise redemption. At the same time, we confess to our own shortcomings, giving the shape of language to our misdeeds. Over and over we repeat a litany of sins, the repetition digging deeper into our souls each time and, progressively, uncovering the reality of our failings. Words spur self-discovery.

Yet the list of sins to which the congregation confesses clearly contains misdeeds *not* committed by most of the congregation. Why should a worshiper stand before God and ask for forgiveness for transgressions that he or she never committed?

The first answer is that this acts as a shield for those who need to confess. When all the congregation lift up their voices and say, "We have sinned by . . ." no one knows who is truly confessing to the misdeed.

Nonetheless there is another, deeper reason. We tend to split ourselves off from those who commit terrible crimes. They seem different in kind. Sometimes this protects us, sometimes it simply serves as an excuse. We turn criminals into monsters and therefore we need not share the sense that they, too, are people. Yet it is precisely the violation of what we share that is so horrible.

Judaism teaches that those who commit terrible deeds are not monsters. They are human beings who have done monstrous things. If they truly were beasts, they would be blameless. They are human, and responsible because they have betrayed their humanness.

We share humanity. It would be possible for us to commit those same terrible crimes in certain situations *if we allowed ourselves to do it*. Therefore we are not allowed to say, "Well, given my character, I could never do such a thing." By confessing to sins we have not committed, we admit that such deeds are possible for us. We do not separate ourselves. We recognize the demonic potential that exists in the most placid breast.

We speak words to understand ourselves, sometimes the deepest pieces of ourselves. In the simple transition from "I" to "we" in the confessional, a world of insight is opened. The words of confession carry tremendous weights of meaning. We confess because confession sears the soul, it opens and exposes us.

All of the self-examination, and even self-flagellation, that occurs in the Yom Kippur confession seems strange at first. Why should people so deride and devalue themselves? But of course the point behind it all is that it is an exaltation of being human, not a devaluation, that is taking place. It is reminiscent of the joke about three scholars who stood in the synagogue during the confessional, beating their breasts and crying out, "I am nothing, I am nothing." A humble unlearned man standing in the back of the synagogue saw the scholars debasing themselves and pleading before God. Seeing the great scholars behave like this, he decided that this was the proper way to pray. So he began beating his breast and screaming, "I am nothing, I am nothing." With disdain, one of the scholars nudged the other, pointed to the man, and said, "Huh! Look who thinks he's nothing!"

The point of that joke is to underline the self-esteem that hides behind saying "I am nothing." You do not say "I'm nothing" unless you think you are something. While in the joke self-esteem spills over into arrogance, in the confessional prayer it is not arrogance, but a healthy sense of value. Were human beings not supremely worthwhile, there would be no point to confessing sin—sin would be expected. In Judaism, worthiness is the indispensable foundation for healthy self-blame.

Words sandblast the self. They reach toward truth, make their way inside us. Much of what we have said about words in Judaism is directed toward the end of discovering the nature of the human relationship not only with God and with others, but also with oneself. What are we truly like, what is inside of us? To strip away the facades of self is the work of a lifetime. The great Chasidic Rabbi of Kotzk, renowned for his human insight and raw honesty, once shouted at his disciples: "Masks! Where are your faces?" Through words, words angry or despairing, he sought to pierce the pretenses of his students cowering behind their masks. We might decide that ultimately the great Rabbi of Kotzk failed, because toward the end of his life he lapsed into a silence that lasted for many years. Yet we remember many of his words, so perhaps his words were more penetrating than his silence. Perhaps.

New Ancient Words

Next to our world, the world of our ancestors was a spare, harsh place. The cushions of modern life, from advanced medicine to electronic diversions, were lacking. Entertainment lay in tales, sustenance in stories. Words grew out of that world, and we might well have thought that they would die with it. What need have we of the stories that men and women told each other thousands of years ago? The desert sands on which they sat weaving tales have long since passed through history's hourglass.

Yet the force, the necessity, of their words carries relevance through the ages. We recall Jeremiah's plea, "I thought 'I will not mention God or speak any more in His name.' But the word was like a raging fire in my heart, shut up in my bones; I tried to hold it in, but I was helpless" (Jer. 20:9). As we might expect, what pours forth from such prophetic compulsion is deeper and truer than casual human utterance. It carries currents of fire. As the *Zohar*, the central text of Jewish mysticism, says occasionally about particularly poignant teachings, these are "new ancient words."

Part of the genius of the word is not only in the speaker, however. The listener must be as brilliant, in his or her way, as the one who speaks. Whitman wrote that for there to be great poems there must be great audiences. Surely part of the greatness of the Torah is the greatness of readers throughout the generations. Ancient stories must be carefully heard, because in listening there is almost as much art, and growth, as in telling. Great listening is in its way no less difficult than great writing. It is simply less cultivated, less noted, less hailed by the world. The Jewish tradition is a tradition of those who could listen with their minds and souls. That is the purpose of a strange phrasing in the first paragraph of the *Sh'ma*, the fundamental declaration of the Jewish prayer service: "... and these words shall be *on* your heart, and you shall teach them diligently to your children." The Rabbis ask why the words should be *on* one's heart, and not *in* one's heart. After all, particularly as the aim is to teach one's children, they should be held inside the heart.

The answer given is that the words *should* be in the heart, but that is not always possible. Sometimes we are not prepared to listen, and our hearts are not always open. At times, when the heart is callous, the words will not be able to penetrate. But if they are placed *on* one's heart, then when the heart softens a bit, when the heart is more receptive, when we are ready to listen, the words will sink inside. The *Sh'ma* seeks to counsel us to listen even when we are disinclined to absorb all that we have heard, to listen with the understanding that words which do not touch us today may change our lives tomorrow.

This passage is pivotal to the prayer service not only because it contains an affirmation of Jewish faith, but because it embodies a central value. The prayer speaks about the possession of tradition *and* the transmission of tradition. We note how that tradition is passed on from generation to generation in the continuation of the *Sh'ma*: "And you shall teach them diligently to your children, speaking of them when you sit in your house, and when you walk by the way, when you lie down, and when you rise up." The first act of transmission is speech: "speaking of them." Actions can speak volumes, but it is equally true that words can summarize lifetimes of action. That is why, even when the prayer continues with action, words are implicated. For the paragraph goes on to say: "... and you shall bind them for a sign upon your hand, and they shall be for frontlets between your eyes. You shall inscribe them on the doorpost of your house and upon your gates."

The frontlets and signs the prayer speaks about are the tefillin, the leather prayer straps, and the mezuzah, the doorpost marker in a Jewish home. Each of these objects contains a scroll of words inside. Even in action we pay homage to the word. The tefillin are bound during prayer next to the mind and heart. Jews are instructed to kiss the mezuzah upon entering a home so adorned.

In the Talmud itself, only three things are called *Tashmishe K'dusha*, objects of holiness: Torah, T'fillin, and the Mezuzah. All three are objects which contain sacred texts. They are holy because they contain holy words, because listening to them is holy.

Judaism perceives a certain stillness, an almost indescribable placidity and perfection, that we can sometimes glimpse behind the turmoil of the world. It is not something we can see or hear, but it can be felt. There is the corner of Eden still tantalizingly in view. Words are the medium for capturing and transmitting that magic sense from one person to another.

Curiously, words are not capable of an absolute description. You cannot sketch the stillness in words. Rather, words can explain it the way that children paint outlines of their hands: by spraying paint around the image and lifting the hand up from the paper, one can see the void that becomes a picture. We cannot describe the perfection at the heart of things, and if we could, it would hardly be believed, given the terrific din of bustle and distress in the world. Yet in describing the activity of the world, in painting around the center of life with words, with depiction and description, the sensitive listener can hear that all words are straining to reach beyond themselves. Words matter so much in Judaism not only because they describe what is, but because they hint at the indescribability of the ultimate reality. As homelessness creates the appreciation of home, the failures of our eloquence foster an appreciation for what we cannot describe. The most excruciating awareness is the awareness of all that defies categorization, the things that lie always beyond the boundaries of language. And paradoxically, the only way to approach them is through words themselves.

The world is real, but it wears a veil.

SIX

~

Babel and Beyond

Preparation of the heart comes from human beings,
but the gift of speech comes from God.

ARESHET S'FATENU

The first great story about human language is the episode of the Tower of Babel. The tale of the tower
(Gen. 11:1–9) tells of the division of humanity by language. In the terse style of the Bible, it proffers an explanation for the immense array of tribes and tongues in the
world.

The tale is one of hubris. At first, "Everyone on earth
had the same language and the same words." That seems
to suggest the possibility of great achievement if this
universal comprehension can be properly harnessed.

However, the people of the time decide to use language
not for self-exploration, but for self-aggrandizement.
Humanity seeks to build a tower to touch the sky and
"make a name for ourselves; else we shall be scattered all
over the world." They do not undertake the task to serve
goodness, nor for art, nor for the pleasure of knowledge.

The tower is the pure, looming product of pride. They believe physical structures will guarantee immortality and unity. In the biblical tale, they are punished for seeking to glorify themselves. The punishment visited upon them is the confusion of tongues. No more would humanity speak in one language.

The story is in part an etiological account—that is, a story of origins. It explains how human beings came to speak in such various ways. Of course, there is also a deeper intent. The story shows how language is at the heart of human connection and distance.

The Rabbis of the Talmud understand different biblical generations to have different characteristics. They call those who built the Tower of Babel *dor Haplagah*—"the generation of separation." We might understand this to mean the generation that endured God's punishment of dispersion, that was separated by God's decree. But perhaps the separation to which the Rabbis refer was more primary.

For this was a generation separate from God. They sought to reach the sky with a tower, and to immortalize themselves. But they did not seek to use their common language to reach out to God. They thought that physical structures were sufficient to reach the heavens. They were indeed a generation of separation, but the separation was of the spirit.

Perhaps God's punishment through language was instructional. In that way they could discover the miraculous tool they had taken for granted. Robbed of a common tongue, the builders of Babel now had to explore what it meant to speak, discover ways in which words could be used to connect with others, and with God. It is no coincidence that the story following Babel is that of Abraham, the first patriarch. Once humanity understood the preciousness of words, the way in which language invests the world with meaning, it could begin to reach toward God.

In Judaism the structure of devotion is not a physical tower. To grasp eternity through spires of stone is a chimera, a delusion. The generation of Babel built the tower, according to the Bible, because they wanted to be famous, and they feared being dispersed over the face of the earth. Fearing physical alienation, they did not understand the deeper, more primary spiritual alienation plaguing them. They did not realize that unity and closeness come not with a skyscraper, but with communication and common understanding.

The tale of Babel reminds us what is really at stake with language. It is about drawing close, and pulling apart. It is about navigating the vast maze of language, sometimes by carefully choosing the road that leads to an opening, sometimes by seeking to break down the walls of the labyrinth and reach the hub of another's heart.

The Tower of Babel is just the beginning of a fascination with the function and meaning of language. Perhaps no other group has seen in language quite the potential and the mystery that the mystics have. In contrast to the generation of separation, they seek to connect to God through words, through letters, and ultimately through silence. The mystics seek to move beyond babel.

Mystic Words

Language has always attracted mystics. There are many reasons for this, not the least of which is the startling magic of language: with a network of sounds, we decipher the world. That act alone should arouse enduring amazement. Imagine recasting all the objects of the world, atoms to stars, into sound, into language! That thought could already begin moving one along a mystical path. By vibration of the vocal cords you can draw a portrait in another's mind. By the schematic splashing of ink on a page, you can communicate the most complex ideas and speak them repeatedly throughout time. Language has its roots in the miraculous. It expands our sense of wonder, and as the mystical classic the *Zohar* explains, God can only be known and grasped to the degree that one opens the gates of imagination.

Above even our own skill with language, remarkable as that is, in Judaism language has a prior and greater function. For in Judaism, the Divine message was cloaked in language. So it is natural that language was envisioned among the mystics as having special properties, as able to unlock secrets, including the secrets of heaven.

The language of mystic speculation was the language of the Bible—Hebrew. Jewish mystics believe Hebrew to have special properties, since in Judaism Hebrew was the language of revelation. To translate Hebrew into any other language, then, is to distort the meaning, to change the values and nuance. Translation loses the very essence of the text. The letters themselves are considered essential to unlocking mysteries. In their peculiar arrangement, even in their shape, lies part of the meaning.

Jewish mysticism has always found messages in letters, in their combination and their numerical values. An early mystical work, *Sefer Yetsirah*, teaches that God created the world with "letters and boundaries." Language is the great generative force; God speaks, and all things come into being. Yet God cannot speak limitlessly, for that would

overwhelm the world and leave no room for human beings, or human enterprise. Along with language, there
must be restriction—God's silence too is part of the creative process. Creativity is thus a function of language and
limitation. Our task is to use both well.

Jewish mysticism urges its adherents to see words as special in a number of ways, many of them bound up with
the question of interpretation. Tradition teaches that the
Torah is subject to several levels of interpretation. One
of the deepest levels of interpretation is the mystical
meaning.

Part of divining the secret meaning is being familiar
with kabbalistic speculation. Although this is not to our
purpose here, we should pause for a moment to discuss
how one arrives at some of that deeper meaning. All letters in Hebrew have a numerical value. (Aleph is one, bet
is two, and so forth.) This dual significance (each letter
also representing a number) is not a mystical idea, but a
property of the Hebrew language, which did not represent
numbers by numerals. However, the tradition took full
advantage of this double meaning, assuming that God's
revelation must contain significance numerically as well as
linguistically. One of the traditional ways of understanding the Torah, therefore, is to count up the values in a
given passage and see, often by quite complicated combinations of numbers, to what these values refer. The
combination of numbers, as well as the subtle interactions
of letters and sounds, plays a part not only in flights of
interpretive ingenuity, but in mystical explanation, even
in mystical visions.

Foreign though this idea may be to moderns, it becomes less outlandish if we recall that God addresses us

in this world through language. To explore language then becomes, in a very circumscribed way, to read the map of God's mind insofar as it is given to us to understand. Some kabbalists extend this idea and see all the world as a reflection of the combination of Hebrew letters. That is to say that although we may *think* we live in a world of things, we really live in a world of letters, and all that exists is language. The world is the language of God, and everything is part of God's expression. Creation and language are intimately bound together. The world is a compendium of language, through which creation occurs. As Rabbi Pinchas of Koritz put it: "The world is like a book that can be read in either direction. There is the power of creation, to make something from nothing. And there is the power of destruction, to make nothing out of something."

To pierce the language of the world, to read the book of all that is, the mystics turned to the source of language, the Torah. They devoted phenomenal care to the reading of the text, in line with the long-established practice of Jewish tradition. The Rabbis advised that we should read the Torah as one reads a love letter: each phrase should be lingered over, wondered about, squeezed for all possible significance. It should be cherished, reread, pondered over and over again. For it is indeed a love letter, a love letter sent by God.

To bring that letter to life is the task of the recipient. In the conjunction of life with language the world awakens. One rabbinic midrash posits that there are 600,000 letters in the entire Torah, recalling the biblical statement that 600,000 people stood at Sinai to receive God's revelation. The letters, asserts the midrash, had been waiting,

waiting for living human beings. The giving of the Torah joined the 600,000 letters with the 600,000 lives. Each letter found a soul to carry out its message. Join language to life, and the result is the word—and the world—of God.

Mystics used the letters in many ways. Some sought to attain visions, even levels of prophecy, by the combination and recitation of certain letters. Mystical meditations focused on specific words, certain letters, various combinations. For example, there was the practice of *tzeruf*, which involves going over a biblical phrase again and again until it loses its plain meaning (the way any word will come to sound alien and bizarre if repeated enough times), combining the letters of various words, and repeating different combinations of letters belonging to the same word. Using these techniques together with particular breathing and other practices, the mystic attained a transformed state. The state could be reached only through the gate of words.

In mystical tradition, the name of God gave great powers to one who knew and could use it. Various mystics based their meditations on the Hebrew names of God in one form or another. Going back to ancient times there was a secret, "ineffable" name of God. In the midrashic account of his death, Moses fights off an angel by brandishing this name of God. Some Jewish mystics sought to harness and use that same power.

This may seem foreign to those of us who assume that language is just a system of sounds. For the kabbalists, language was and is much more. Language was a weapon and a shield. It was the mystic cord that bound people to each other and to previous generations. It was the medium of understanding the world and the medium of connection with the Divine.

~

One way of evaluating a life is to ask not only its content, but its direction: toward what does one reach? What is the aim of aspiration? Some reach toward particular possessions. Their hands are skilled at grasping material goods. Others reach toward those close to them, those whom they cherish. Their arms enfold, holding loved ones close. Still others reach inside, exploring their own workings. They become masters of meditation and introspection. The mystics reach toward God. To ascend is the totality of their quest. All other motion in their lives is a piece of the ultimate movement, which is upward. This motion leads most Jewish mystics not to leave the world, but to dwell *inside* it, to feel its reality differently, to experience people differently, still as part of the same world that all inhabit. While there were Jewish mystics who sought isolation, most dwelt in the world and tried to find a path not out, but through.

To realize such a quest one needs exceptional means. The usual instruments will not do. The mystics wielded a powerful tool, the tool of language. Since the quest was so difficult, the goal so remote, they had to forge language into a particularly powerful medium, seeing in it a force far beyond the words of daily conversation.

Certain features of the mystical quest are unique. Nonetheless, mysticism has something to teach about the heart of Judaism, and about all spiritual search. The mystics built on the foundation of religious language. They took the classical texts of Judaism and tried to take their words in new directions. Animated by spiritual hunger, the mystics sought more unfailingly, more raptly, what so many before and after them also sought: an expansion of the self, a deeper connection to this world, an elevated understanding of the Divine.

A mystical prayer teaches that the world was formed by letters descending to earth. It is our task to take those letters, form them into words, and send them back to their Source, back to God. Prayer is the culmination of creation. There will one day come a point when this circular process will end, and the silence of perfect understanding will reign. Until then we make what progress we can with words of the mind, and of the heart.

Words of the Mind

In many traditional Jewish communities, when a child entered *cheder*, religious school, for the first time, that child was greeted by a curious sight: a chart of letters smeared with honey. The new student licked off the honey from the letters, one by one, thus learning a critical lesson: learning is sweet, and the very letters of the words carry the sweetness.

Study is so sweet because it is wresting meaning from the world. Making things yield their sense in language is the aim of study. One seeks to understand, always to understand, whether it is the intricate talmudic argument or the idea behind a lovely legend. The words explain, and conceal. One can view the world as a work of art, as a pageant, as a tragedy, as a comedy, as a farce; all of these may be true, but the Jewish tradition also sees the world in another light—the world is a riddle. And the aim of this earth's inhabitants is to figure it out.

That is why there is such intense concentration on the

transmission of tradition from one generation to the next. There are answers for each generation to work out on its own, but if it loses the accumulated answers of all previous generations, then it must start at the beginning. Why work to arrive at the same point as those who preceded us? The goal is to build, to expand the net of language until it takes in more and more of the world, until we snare more bits of meaning in the grillwork of our concepts. There is tearing down to be done as well as building up, but even in tearing down it is well to keep the shattered fragments on hand; one never knows when more material will be required for the new structure.

A wonderful and real-life metaphor for this preservation exists in the way Judaism has traditionally disposed of sacred texts. Since holy books cannot be destroyed, they are placed in a *genizah*, which is a depository, almost like a grave, for sacred texts that can no longer be used. Thousands of works that contain the name of God— prayer books, marriage contracts, written oaths, strips from prayer shawls and tefillin, other bits of sacred script—find their way into a *genizah*.

Some *genizot* (plural of *genizah*) have existed for hundreds of years. The most famous among them is from Egypt, the *genizah* of the great synagogue in Cairo, which in the early part of this century yielded an almost unimaginable treasure trove of documents reaching back over a thousand years. Almost one hundred years after its discovery, scholars are still poring through and cataloguing the riches of this extraordinary find.

The scholar most responsible for the work on the Cairo *genizah* manuscripts was Solomon Schechter. Schechter, upon entering the great *genizah*, beheld an ancient warehouse of words where the jumble of the ages was tossed together: documents of indebtedness were wrapped around moralistic tracts warning against borrowing and lending money; sanctified, sober prayer books were welded from the force of years to superstitious charms and amulets.

In this catacomb of language, a sepulcher for words, we can see the search for understanding and the reverence for writing so characteristic of Judaism. First and foremost is the impulse not to destroy the written sanctity of God's name. But we may also see the drive to preserve. Not a scrap must escape or be lost to history. The possibility remains that some neglected shred may contain the answer to a pressing question, a question of history, of law, of interpretation, of life. Do not forget the words, exhorts Moses. Remember. To remember the words is to remember the lives. To remember the words is to remember the meaning. To remember the words is to remember God.

In the early part of this century, a great Jewish philosopher named Franz Rosenzweig wrote a book called *The Star of Redemption*. In it he developed the idea of "speech thinking." For Rosenzweig, the detached method of sitting silently and turning over abstract concepts in the privacy of one's mind is too remote from life as it is lived. Thinking alone, which we usually identify with "philosophy," is a rather unnatural way for human beings to explore. In dialogue, in exchange, in the heat of speech one uncovers truths of life. As we speak we affirm things we did not know we believed. We deny propositions we had previously thought to be true. As the novelist E. M. Forster once remarked, "How do I know what I think 'till I see what I say?" In contact with other minds, other words, our own worldview emerges. In dialogue is discovery.

This relational, verbal way of approaching truth is profoundly rooted in Judaism. In the Bible, God and the children of Israel are engaged in a dialogue, a mutual search. Indeed, we read in the book of Isaiah that when humanity does not participate in the exchange, God is grieved: "Why, when I came, was no one there? Why, when I called, would none respond?" (50:2).

For Rosenzweig as for the Jewish tradition, the ragged, uncertain process of encounter, in which two beings seek each other's essence, occurs through the medium of speech. Sometimes that search is between people, sometimes between the individual or the community and God. The process cannot be predicted in advance, however, because the dialogue is dynamic, asymmetrical, exciting. In the dialogue with God, the individual is shaped, changed, begins to grow in ways that seemed impossible before. From the words preserved in dusty anterooms, to the heated dialogue of philosophers, Judaism seeks to move beyond Babel. Each word is a rung on the ladder of spirit; each word, shaped and refined by the mind, originates in the heart.

Words of the Heart

For if they see with their eyes, hear with their ears,
and understand with their hearts, they will repent
and be healed.

ISA. 6:10

Prayer is a pouring forth of the human soul. The devotional words, repeated throughout the generations, chronicle our hopes, our thanks, our desire to be heard, and our fear that we are not really heard. Almost all who pray must wonder at times if prayer is but an idle, unnoticed gesture. The history of human heartache can also be read as a history of unheeded prayers. If we could gather up all those prayers from the crevices of the universe and the corners of time, and place them in a book, it would make the most wrenching reading imaginable. What aggrieved soul or affrighted spirit has not at some moment offered up a prayer? To see the prayers of humanity is to see all that we wished for, and all that has befallen us. It is to see all the disappointments, all the dreams that did not come true. To hear the prayers of the world is to see the heart-scars of humanity.

What is the value of those words, piled atop one another, words plaintive, pitiful, imploring? Taken together, what are they supposed to mean?

Images of prayer in the Jewish tradition suggest that it is communication that softens, opens, deepens us. As the Hebrew proverb has it, "Words that come from the heart, enter the heart."

Prayer cannot be spoken from a heart that is hardened. Words should unlock the spirit. That is why when the Bible speaks of the words of God, it does not advise that they be engraved on tablets of stone: "Write them," reads the verse in Proverbs, "on the tablet of your heart" (7:3). We are reminded in a famous verse that the heart upon which one inscribes them must not itself be of stone "I will remove the heart of stone from their bodies and give them a heart of flesh" (Ezek. 11:19). It was this prophetic image that moved a modern poet to reflect, looking on the Western Wall of the Temple, stuffed with the written pleas of a people, "There are people with hearts of stone, and stones with the hearts of human beings."

Through genuine interchange we begin to understand

how different it is to hear with one's ears and to hear with one's heart. There is a charming biblical tale recounting Samuel's first encounter with God. He is a boy, in the service of Eli, the High priest. One night, as he lay on his bed,

> The Lord called out to Samuel, and he answered, "I'm coming." He ran to Eli and said, "Here I am, you called me." But Eli replied, "I didn't call you; go back to sleep." So he went back and lay down. Again the Lord called, "Samuel!" Samuel rose and went to Eli and said, "Here I am; you called me." But he replied, "I didn't call, my son; go back to sleep." —Now Samuel had not yet experienced the Lord; the word of the Lord had not yet been revealed to him. —The Lord called Samuel again, a third time, and he rose and went to Eli and said, "Here I am; you called me." Then Eli understood that the Lord was calling the boy. And Eli said to Samuel, "Go lie down. If you are called again, say, 'Speak, Lord, for Your servant is listening.' " And Samuel went to his place and lay down.
>   The Lord came, and stood there, and He called as before: "Samuel! Samuel!" And Samuel answered, "Speak, for Your servant is listening." (1 Samuel 3:4–10)

Part of the charm of the tale is Samuel's naïveté. But the telling sentence "Now Samuel had not yet experienced the Lord; the word of the Lord had not yet been revealed to him" explains more than naïveté. Samuel did not understand that the voice belonged to God, because it seemed so ordinary. He took it for Eli's voice, for surely the voice of God would be accompanied by awesome signs, by peals of thunder. Samuel's lack of experience was his failure to realize that God does not speak in earsplitting declarations, but in subtle messages to the heart. Samuel was listening in the casual manner of a boy often called to menial tasks. He needed to open his heart, and that had to be from conscious choice. God's call to Samuel is insistent, but it is not overpowering.

The lesson is manifest: God will not hurl pronouncements from the sky such that people must listen. As is evident from the history of our world, a characteristic of God is that God grants us the option to ignore. We need not heed the Divine. Whether God hears prayer is something that can only be answered deep inside us, in that place where the soul is still enough to hear how God speaks to human beings in this world—in a whisper, the whisper of conscience, the whisper of direction and guidance. The more important and private a communication, the more one inclines to speak softly, so that it is heard only by the intended listener. If we think this way of God's communication in the world, the whisper must be soft indeed. For the message is addressed differently to each human heart, and its import is great. So the words, soft, solitary, are like breezes that move through us, to play out each personal melody on the gently vibrating strings of the soul.

Strange as it may sound, the ultimate aim of prayer, at most times, is not to ask, nor to be answered. The aim of prayer is to pray. The aim of speaking to God is the aim of speaking to other human beings, which is not to transmit information, nor to elicit a particular response. Those are the secondary purposes. The final aim of prayer is to express oneself, to seek understanding, to bring forth out of the inchoate and jumbled bits of the self an expression of what is real, and what is true. Prayer to God, like deep speech to other human beings, is an offering. And the deepest need of one who makes an offering is to offer.

Prayer is a process of self-discovery, by which the storm of a self pours forth. Prayer is unbinding. It is in *tefillah*, in prayer, that a turbulent spirit can say what it wishes, and what it needs.

Prayer serves not only the uneasy, but the one who is tranquil, who needs to express gratitude for the beauty of the world or the blessed calmness of the soul. Much of prayer is joy given rhythm and direction—it is a celebration pitched toward the heavens. Some prayers are the throb of pain seeking utterance and alleviation. Others are looking for wings to carry bliss.

"Hear O Israel." You must listen. The world is poised on the edge of the word.

One word, a single word, can spin a world on its axis. Interpretation is a daring adventure because of this marvelous feature of speech. Everything hangs upon a word. In rabbinic writings, there is a wonderful example from the story of Abraham, at the very beginning of the search for God.

In the Bible, we see that God comes and speaks to Abraham and exhorts him to leave home on a journey. We are not told, however, how Abraham came to recognize this Being as God. How did Abraham arrive at the overpowering idea that one God ruled the universe? Living in a world rife with idolatry and paganism, what insight did this lone shepherd achieve that raised him above the assumptions of his age?

The Midrash tells a number of stories of Abraham's search. Some of them are fanciful and even humorous. Perhaps best known is the legend that Abraham's father, Terach, was an idol-maker, and one night Abraham, entrusted to watch over the workshop, smashed all his father's idols. In the morning, his father angrily upbraided him: "What have you done to my livelihood?" Abraham calmly replied, "It wasn't me. The idols had a fight with each other." Enraged, Terach said, "What are you talking about? They can't fight with each other. They are made of wood and stone!" Abraham nodded and asked, "Then why, Father, do you worship them?"

This story does not tell us, however, *how* Abraham arrived at this conviction about idols. We still do not know why he decided to dissent from the world in which he was raised. Another midrash offers the following analogy. Abraham's story may be compared to a traveler who saw a magnificent palace on fire. Seeing the fire, he cried out, "Is there no one to care for this place?" The owner peeked his head out of the window and said, "The palace is mine, and I am taking care of it. Do not fear."

The analogy is clear. Abraham saw the horror of much of what occurs in the world and cried out to the heavens, "Is there no one to take care of this world?" God then appeared to Abraham and reassured him: "I am watching over the world; do not fear."

But the marvel of the midrash is in the phrase "on fire." The word in Hebrew for "on fire" is *doleket*. Yet *doleket* can also mean "full of light." In that case, the midrash bears a very different meaning. Now Abraham saw the world not as consumed by flames, but as filled with light, stunning and splendid. Struck by its beauty, he called out, "Does no one care for this place?" And God responded from the heavens, "Do not fear. It is mine and I care for it."

The story contains both a religious and a psychological truth. Some see the world as filled with pain and tragedy, and come to God out of a sense of the terrific wants of this life. Others see the radiance of the world and come to God out of appreciation. Some dispositions see light, others fire. Either way, we now know why Abraham came to a belief in God. It was through a deep and penetrating appreciation of the nature of the world. Abraham felt its pain, cherished its joy. That insight led him to God.

Two entire worldviews are wrapped up in the interpretation of one word, *doleket*. Turn the word on one side and there is fire; on the other, there is crystalline light. Perhaps the midrash intends to teach us both, that the world is full of beauty, but also full of pain, and that both in their way can lead us to God.

It all hangs upon a word.

SEVEN

~

Tears

Even when the gates of heaven are closed to prayer,
they are open to tears.

RABBI ELEAZAR BEN PEDAT

So much depends upon language that words seem
sometimes to represent the whole range of human
meanings. Yet we know that action, gesture, ritual, and
rite also embody great truths. There are moments when
spoken expression simply cannot convey the passion in a
soul. When words fail us, when we can neither sing nor
speak, there are tears.

One of the gates of childhood through which all pass
is the gate of tears. Tears prove essential in the first years
of life not only to communicate before we have learned
language, but also to signify that which will never yield
to utterance. Tears represent another, often deeper, level
of expression. "There is a palace," it is recorded in *Tikkune
Zohar*, "that opens only for tears."

To a greater or lesser extent, many of us lose the ability
to cry, that spontaneous burst of visible pain that tears

represent. To be unable to cry bespeaks a tremendous loss. For expressions of both joy and sorrow, tears well up from a site words cannot reach.

Once again if we turn to the Jewish tradition we discover a stunning depiction of the place of tears in human life. The overflow of human feeling has always given way to weeping. We are hardly the first people that wept, or needed to.

It is evident that tears mattered for our ancestors; in the Bible they are crucial. In an earlier chapter we considered the terrible resentment Esau felt for his brother Jacob. After years of estrangement in which the brothers hated and feared each other, Jacob and Esau are finally reunited. Their encounter is drenched in tears. They fall on each other's neck and weep for all the wasted years twisted by hate and blackened by needless enmity. Jacob and Esau were twins. They were not identical, but they were born within moments of each other, and the total length of their lives was of one piece. Because they were of the same age when each looked into the face of his brother after such a long separation, it must have been like looking into a mirror. Seeing each other after twenty years, both Jacob and Esau must have been struck: each struck by how old the other had grown, and therefore how old he himself had grown.* The agonizing loss of decades laced with hatred was etched in each line of the brothers' faces. How many years had animosity poisoned their lives? All the wasted years found reflection in their eyes. Could any words serve to encompass such a loss? They wept.

Later on, Jacob's son Joseph is sold into slavery by his

---

*I owe this beautiful insight into the Jacob and Esau story to my father, Rabbi Gerald Wolpe.

own brothers. He grows to adulthood in Egypt, far from his family, his land, and his language. Eventually the despised brother becomes the viceroy of Egypt. He encounters his older siblings for the first time in years when they arrive to buy grain during a famine. Seeing them again, Joseph is overcome. He turns away and weeps. So loud was his weeping, recounts the Bible, that all of Egypt could hear the sobs that poured forth from this man whose power was second only to that of Pharaoh in all the land of Egypt.

Repeatedly in the Bible we see that figures of great strength, figures of faith, pour out their souls in tears. Eloquent though they can be, words are not always sufficient to tap the pathos that lies beneath the surface of the everyday. As God says to a repentant King Hezekiah, "I have heard your prayer, I have seen your tears" (Isa. 38:4). Sometimes words are the prelude; the only thing that can tell the truth is tears.

In the book of Samuel, David, soon to be king, weeps on the shoulder of his friend Jonathan when he has to flee from the wrath of Jonathan's father, Saul. In years to come, David will cry even more bitterly at the death of his own son Absalom. David, who was a musician, a poet, a Psalmist, had not lost that bit of himself which enabled him to experience, understand, and express pain. This supremely capable man found the world at times overwhelming. David did not use the cloak of the monarch to hide from himself. Kings too can weep.

These tears are not incidental to the characters of Jacob, Esau, Joseph, and David. They express a surfeit of pain and demonstrate a readiness to pour out sufferings in a medium that can be deeper than words. Tears are a reflection of the fullness of feeling, which overflows the bounds of normal speech.

Of course, the need to weep did not end in the Bible. We learn from the Talmud that each year the High Priest, the day before he was to enter the Holy of Holies in the Temple to pray for the people, would spend the evening with the elders of Israel. They would remind him of the responsibilities he bore for all the people. The High Priest would weep, and the elders would cry with him. If he could not weep, he was not worthy.

That the High Priest is expected to cry shows how far Judaism is from the assumption that crying is unmanly, or simply inconsequential. Tears are both a release and a reflection of the essential soundness of the personality. Worry and sorrow should overflow; one of the names given for a cemetery in the Talmud is a "field of tears." To be unable to weep is an indication of weakness, not sturdiness; evidence of fear, not of faith. The Jewish tradition well understands the wisdom of the poet Dante, who, in his *Inferno*, made the inability to cry one of the punishments of the damned.

That torture is one that many share. Crying makes us feel lost. It can be difficult, if not impossible, to crack the reserve inside that shields our tears. Something must part to leave a pathway open through which the tears can flow, and there is always the fear that when we open something inside it will remain exposed, easily wounded. Weeping seems such an admission—that we cannot handle the world, that we are children inside, that we are less than we ought to be. It seems as if the cry is a shortcoming, and if we were better, we could navigate this world with strength and continual calm. Then we turn again to the Bible and discover that even in the character of its greatest hero, its most powerful personality, there is a cry at the center of the soul.

The Cry of Moses

In exploring problems that Moses had with words and with speech, we noted that his life begins with a cry. The Bible informs us of this in an awkward and uncharacteristic way. We read: "The daughter of Pharaoh came down to bathe in the Nile, while her maidens walked along the Nile. She spied the basket among the reeds and sent her slave girl to fetch it. When she opened it, she saw that it was a child, a boy crying. She took pity on it ..." (Exod. 2:5, 6).

Curiously, the Bible speaks of Pharaoh's daughter seeing, not hearing, Moses' cry. The explanation for this given by some commentators is that Moses did not cry aloud. His cry was of the deepest kind—silent. It was *azur mimaamake halev*—stopped up in the depths of his heart, and all the sadness and terror he felt was reflected on his face. The expression on Moses' face, the eloquence of his agony, the refusal to cry aloud, moved Pharaoh's daughter so much that she adopted the child and brought him up in Pharaoh's palace.

According to this view, the reason Moses could not cry aloud was that it was not safe. Moses could not behave normally; children were under a decree of death, and he was surrounded by danger. Had he been discovered he would, as a Hebrew child, have been killed. His cry had to be curbed, his tears restrained, his voice remain low. To survive even as an infant, Moses could not cry like a child.

This is the understanding of tears that suggests they

are withheld because of a sense of danger. In expressing our feelings we are too vulnerable, not in the physical sense of a Moses, but in a spiritual and emotional sense. The admission of tears is dangerous.

That is the explanation of one commentator of this story. But there is a midrash that teaches the precise opposite. It is true that Moses was retraining his cries. How then, muses the midrash, was it that Pharaoh's daughter spotted the basket? There must have been some sound. Surely more than pure coincidence drew her to the child. As much as Moses tried to restrain his cry, it must have been possible for Pharaoh's daughter to hear him, or he would have remained abandoned. The midrashist imagines that an angel was sent from heaven to save Moses; he gently struck the baby so that Moses cried. Pharaoh's daughter heard, and rescued him.

This midrash teaches something else about tears. They save as often as they endanger, and at times it is the fear of crying itself, the tight rein we put on our own heart and guts, that risks hurting us. Strange as it may sound, God sent an angel not to dry Moses' tears, but to encourage them. Weeping was not the danger. The peril lay in being unable to weep.

Hidden in the story of Moses is one more stirring comment on the potency of tears. Surely part of the veneration accorded Moses in the Jewish tradition is because he is seen as a figure not only of strength and resolution, but of tenderness and of love. Part of that image is formed at the very moment that he first appears, a child, crying by the riverbank. For the rest of Moses' life, tears play a part. According to the Midrash, when Moses first stepped out to see the burdens of Israel, he wept. Moses felt the pain of his people, and cried for them. Despite his years of separation, of growing up in the palace of royalty and not among the sufferers, Moses has not lost that sense of sadness which marked him from infancy.

At Moses' death the theme of tears recurs. For the Rabbis teach that following his death, not only did the children of Israel cry, but his disciple Joshua, unable to find his teacher and realizing that he was gone forever, began to cry, and then the heavens cried, and the earth cried. Finally, having taken Moses' soul away with a kiss, even God wept. A universe awash in tears is an eloquent tribute to Moses, who lived with a consciousness of the pain that was a part of the beginning of his own life.

These tears of Moses' are the reflection in one man of the core sorrow in the biblical tale. Moses weeps because of the tribulations of those whom he loves, his people. His tears, joined with those of the children of Israel, are instrumental in ending slavery. Why does God liberate the Jews from Egypt? The Bible recounts: "The Israelites were groaning under the bondage and cried out; and their cry for help from bondage rose up to God. God heard their cries . . ." (Exod. 2:23, 24). Tears were the precursor to liberation.

The Weeping God

The Jewish tradition, which has seen its share of difficulties and tragedy, has a still more eloquent and dramatic example of the power of tears. From time to time in the Midrash, the rabbinic legends, God weeps. Often God weeps for the actions of human beings. Sometimes God weeps for the actions God feels constrained to take in this world.

The tales of God's weeping are commonly clustered

around the greatest tragedy in Jewish history until modern times, the destruction of the Temple. There were two Temples in Jewish history, and two destructions. The first was destroyed by the Babylonians in 586 B.C.E., and the second by the Romans in 70 C.E. Poignantly, the tales we have concerning God's weeping relate to the first Temple, but they were written after the destruction of the second. So the midrash on the biblical book of Lamentations reflects a contemporary pain retrojected onto the past. The Rabbis of the Talmud, standing amid the rubble of their own society, their own hopes, imagine what it must have been like when that first Temple, more than five hundred years before, was razed.

And what they imagine is that when the Temple was destroyed, God cried:

> At the moment that the Temple was destroyed, God began to cry, and lament "Woe is Me! What have I done! I dwelt below, on earth, for the sake of Israel and now that they have sinned I have removed Myself. . . ." At that moment Metatron [a legendary angel] came and fell upon his face before God and said: "Master of the Universe, let me cry, but don't you cry."

The angel cannot tolerate seeing God's sadness. It pains him, and he will do anything—including take the burden upon himself—to prevent God's shedding tears. But God's response is equally dramatic:

> "If you seek to prevent Me from crying here, I will simply find another place where you cannot approach, and cry there."

God will not be prevented from weeping. Now the midrash continues with an extraordinary journey. The prophet Jeremiah is summoned before God. Seized with grief at the destruction of the Temple and the death and dispersion of Israel, God is not satisfied that Jeremiah grasps the magnitude of the loss. God speaks as follows to the prophet:

> God said to Jeremiah: "I am like a man who has an only child, who prepared a wedding canopy for his child only to have the child die beneath the canopy. Don't you ache for me, and for my child, the people Israel? Go—summon up the souls of Abraham, Isaac, Jacob and Moses from their graves. They knew how to cry."

God's child is the people, and the wedding canopy is the Temple, under which the people are dying. In this tremendously graphic image, we appreciate the force of God's anguish. Seeking the pity of human beings, God asks particularly for their tears. Jeremiah is rebuked in this passage because he does not feel enough pain for the suffering of God! Agonized, God is searching for the sympathy of human beings. In the process, God proposes an interesting criterion for a Jewish leader, a criterion distinguishing the greatest of them: a true leader must know how to cry.

The midrash continues: Jeremiah calls up the souls of the patriarchs. He pretends that he does not know why they are being summoned, for he is frightened of being reproached. After all, he was the leader of the generation. Why did he not prevent the people's sin, which resulted in such a wrenching catastrophe? Jeremiah's sense of failure weighs heavy on him, and he feels overshadowed by the great figures who preceded him. Finally, however, he gathers together Abraham, Isaac, and Jacob, the patriarchs. Then he proceeds to awaken Moses:

> Upon arising and being told of the tragedy that had befallen his people, Moses wailed and cried until he reached the patriarchs. Immediately they tore their clothing [a sign of mourning], placed their hands upon their heads and began wailing and weeping as they journeyed from one end of the conquered city to the other, until they reached the gates of the destroyed Temple. Immediately upon seeing them God mourned and wept and lamented "Woe to the King who triumphs in His youth and fails in His old age."

The patriarchs share God's pain. They march together through the streets crying and wailing for the destruction wreaked upon the land and the people. God, seeing the patriarchs and recalling the earlier days of Israel when things were better, when the people were young and devoted, mourns and cries out, "Woe to the King who triumphs in His youth and fails in His old age." God recalls the triumphs of an earlier generation, the triumphs of liberation from Egypt, and of the initial revelation at Sinai. Years have passed, God is older, and the people are destroyed and dispersed. The only possible response to that is to cry: even as an "old King," God turns to the earliest expression of grief—weeping. While it is true that the Rabbis do not intend this to be literally understood—God does not "age" and to speak of God's crying is a poetic vision, not a verity—the force of tears is so great in life that the Rabbis ascribe them even to God. A God who loves, who understands, cannot be a complete stranger to the tears with which we human beings are endowed to express our joy, our frustration, and at times our devastation.

Tears play such an important role in the Bible and the Jewish tradition in part because of historical suffering. The touchstone of catastrophe, as the midrash above demonstrates, was the destruction of the Temple and the exile. At such a time it seems that the world itself cries out: indeed, the Bible depicts the city of Jerusalem as weeping: "Sorely she weeps in the night, her cheeks wet with tears. There is none to comfort her of all her friends. All her allies have betrayed her; they have become her foes" (Lam. 1:2).

The matriarch Rachel, known in Jewish tradition for her compassion, is recalled in a moving passage from the book of Jeremiah as she watches her children exiled from their land: "A cry is heard on the heights, wailing, and bitter tears. Rachel is weeping for her children. She refuses to be comforted for her children who are no more" (Jer. 31:15).

God, hearing Rachel's cry, seeks to reassure her: "Restrain your voice from weeping, your eyes from shedding tears; for . . . they shall return from the enemy's land. And there is hope for your future—declares the Lord: Your children shall return to their country" (Jer. 31:16, 17).

Notwithstanding tragedy, our need to weep is more elemental than the vagaries and cruelties of history. Judaism reflects the truth of human life. So long as we do not deaden our souls, we each have a cry wrapped up inside of ourselves, a cry that cannot be completely erased. Our first articulation, as with Moses in the biblical tale, is a cry. The rabbinic tradition teaches that the first cry of the child is not accidental. In the journey from eternity to earth, the child has lost a world of perfection. Suddenly introduced into this temporal and difficult world, who would not cry? Indeed, in some Jewish mystical circles, weeping was seen as part of a way to communicate with the Divine. The practice of crying is tied to ascent toward God. Tears can reacquaint the yearning soul with its Maker.

The inability to cry, to pour out pain, is a grotesque result of a misshaped idea of adulthood. "The young man," wrote the philosopher Santayana, "who will not cry is a savage; the old man who cannot laugh is a fool." Adulthood should express the full range of human sentiment, not some narrowed parody of sensitivity. We must be able to laugh and to cry. When life is absurd, or comical, or merry, when the world flashes its brittle lightness, we laugh. When pain knots our throats, when the world presents its brutal face, the Jewish tradition counsels that we imitate God. That we weep.

There are times when tears are one step beyond words on the path to God. Commenting on a biblical passage commanding sacrifices, the Midrash imagines Israel looking up at the heavens and telling God they are too poor to offer sacrifices in expiation for sin. God responds to Israel, "I long for your words. Speak words of Torah I will pardon you." In response, Israel proclaims that its condition is so desperate that they do not even have words of Torah. "Then pray," says God, "and weep, and I will forgive." Tears are important on the path to God, but they are

not the ultimate goal. Eventually tears of sadness and sacrifice should give way to something better. Each of us
aspires to the day when tears of sorrow will no longer be
part of life, an aspiration that is reflected in the promise
of the prophet Isaiah that one day "My Lord God will
wipe the tears away from all faces" (Isa. 25:8).

That notion is so strong that the Rabbis contend, based
on a verse in Jeremiah, that the world will be redeemed
through tears. Through the weeping and repentance of
humanity, the world will be changed forever. The verse
in Jeremiah reads: "They shall come with weeping, and
with compassion I shall lead them" (31:9). When the final
bliss of the world arrives, in this biblical reassurance, it
will be bathed in tears. But they will be changed from
tears of remorse to cries of celebration.

Weeping uncovers a tender part of the self, a part that
seeks comfort, that hopes for healing. Repeatedly the
Jewish tradition insists that tears are but the prelude to
happiness. It is important to remember, because charac-
teristically, Judaism refuses to surrender to despair. As the
Psalmist writes, "They who sow in tears shall reap in joy"
(Ps. 126:5). Isaiah prophesies of that magic time when
God will wipe the tears away from all faces, "On that
day, a song shall be sung" (Isa. 26:1). All tears, one day,
will turn to song.

EIGHT

~

Song

I sing hymns and weave songs because my soul longs for Thee.

SHIR HAKAVOD

Words given wing become song, and the Jewish tradition is borne on wings.

The Hebrew word for song, *shir*, denotes more than musical song; it means poetry, lyric, the use of words that seek to overbound the everyday, to ratchet language up to a different level, to celebrate and explore. To sing is to elevate the ordinary. A song is a statement made sublime.

The Psalmist is all song: "Awake, O harp and lyre! I will rouse the dawn!" (Ps. 108:3). The entire book of Psalms is a collection of songs to God, sometimes angry, often frustrated or even despairing, but usually filled with a sense of exultation and exaltation. Psalms are the melodies of the religious soul put to words.

The Jewish tradition teaches that most of the Psalms were written by King David. The attribution adds poignancy to those remarkable poems. They are not the product of someone removed from the rough-and-tumble of life. These songs are not ornaments of a quiet soul contemplating the world distant from the hum of the marketplace. The Psalms are steeped in the real world of human beings. Their texture is the coarse-grained substance of lessons wrung from experience, from struggle and survival.

In the book of Samuel, the picture of King David is one of vitality and strength. His character bursts from the pages. Through the artistry of the author and the intensity of his subject, we see the rich personality of the king. David was a warrior, his life filled with battles against enemies from outside his kingdom and from within his own court, even within his own family.

For better or worse, David cannot escape political intrigue. The world about him and his own sense of mission do not permit meditative calm. King David, from his youth, is marked by enterprise, keenness, resolve.

Yet David was also a poet. He must have written in snatched time, in the interstices between battles. During his reign, the land of Israel was secured through military campaign. David finally beat back the constant, terrorizing threat of the Philistines. For all that, he is not remembered primarily for conquest. What mark David's reign in the memory of his descendants are the traits of the Psalms: poetry, passion, and faith.

Other kings in the Bible were successful in the way sovereigns of the ancient world are usually measured. They secured their borders, survived intrigues, helped the country to prosper. Yet the Bible does not venerate them. Omri ruled Israel for twelve years and founded a dynasty that ruled Israel for fifty more. His kingship is described in only six verses. For "Omri did what was displeasing to the Lord" (1 Kings 16:25). Political accomplishments alone are not the measure of a leader. The Bible will not esteem political skill if it is not in the service of God. Piety, not power, marks the ideal; not strength alone, but strength allied to song.

King David captured the imagination of his people. His legacy was rich and enduring. In David's prayers, in the Psalms, his very being seeks to become a paean to God. The literal translation of Psalm 109:4 is "I am a prayer."

David sang songs. The people loved him, and they loved him not simply because he represented strength, but because his was the music of the spirit. The quintessential King was a master of melody; he is the "sweet singer of Israel" (2 Sam. 23:1).

David was first introduced to the court of Israel by his predecessor, Saul. Saul suffered from bouts of melancholy. When the dismal moods attacked him, he would feel sad, even terrified. Saul was told of a young man who could coax music from the strings of the harp and perhaps chase away the king's terror. David was brought to the court, and played for the king. Hearing him, Saul's spirit lifted. Ultimately the pressures of kingship and the weaknesses of his character conspired to destroy Saul. In the end, he went mad. But for a while, the song of David kept the beleaguered king sane.

In the Bible, and later in the Talmud, song threads its way through David's life. Using the Psalms as guideposts, the Rabbis chart the rich inner life of the king. They note that David must have arisen in the middle of the night in order to praise God, since the Psalms read, "I arise at midnight to praise You" (Ps. 119:62). The Talmud wonders how the king could be sure of being up at night. The answer is a lovely image that combines devotion and song. Each evening David would hang his harp above his bed. In the middle of the night, a breeze would come and vibrate the strings of the harp, which woke the king with its gentle music.

David's joy before God expressed itself not only in song, but in dance. After the capture of the ark of God by the Philistines, David recovered it in war and returned it to Israel amid celebration. David himself "leaped and whirled" before God. His own wife, Michal, thinking such a display beneath the dignity of the king, despised him for the public fervor of his worship. But the Rabbis, heedless of the rigid dignity of kingship, caring far more for the joyous, fervent revelry of true prayer, praise David's open exhilaration. For the Jewish tradition, it is an ideal—a king who would dance.

For David, song was not only praise and celebration, but succor in times of hardship. The Rabbis note that while there is a Psalm with the superscription "A Psalm of David in the Wilderness," there is no Psalm that begins "A Psalm of David in His Kingship." His songs were balms to a frightened soul, particularly in the days when his predecessor Saul sought to kill him, when David was surrounded by enemies. As tears seem naturally linked to sorrow, but are equally potent as expressions of joy, David teaches us song not only as an outpouring of joy, but as a natural consolation in times of trouble.

King David is the human embodiment of song in the Bible, but the tradition of song is deeper than his kingship, and prior to it. For the whole biblical story swings on the hinge of song: the song the Israelites sang as they escaped from Egypt. The realization that song is the pivot of faith begins at the very moment of Israel's liberation.

The Israelites had been enslaved for hundreds of years. Suddenly, miraculously, they are free. After the dazzling succession of wonders, a people long used to oppression and captivity finds itself marching triumphantly from Egypt. We must imagine what it meant to this ragged band of slaves to be suddenly liberated. The disorientation, the dizziness, of freedom must have made them feel like a spun top. Whirling around, unsure of their direction, they made their way toward the sea. To be abruptly confronted with the barrier of the sea must have been a snap back into reality from the ludicrous dream of freedom. The path had seemed clear, but now the sea blocked any possibility of escape. Reality reasserted itself. They would once again be slaves.

The end of joy always bears the stamp of authenticity. Somehow we cannot believe in happiness, but its abrupt cessation is intense and real. Disillusion and disappointment bear the whiff of truth. Of course they could not really be free. Liberty was obviously a dream, and the return of slavery imminent, inevitable.

Then something happened. The sea split and the bewildered Israelites found themselves safe. Their enemies were vanquished. The future had regained its possibility, and the past would remain firmly past, forever. They were free.

The Bible then reads: "And when Israel saw the wondrous power which the Lord had wielded against the Egyptians, the people revered the Lord; they had faith in the Lord and His servant Moses. Then Moses and the Israelites sang this song to the Lord" (Exod. 14:31, 15:1). In the Midrash, Rabbi Abbahu counsels us to take note of the sequence of events. First the children of Israel come to faith in God. Then, armed with faith, they burst into song.

Faith is the spine of song. When in doubt, they were hushed. Now they have seen, and they believe. Reassured, they can sing. Song is the effusion of faith.

What do the children of Israel sing? "The Lord is my strength and my song—and has become my salvation" (Exod. 15:2). At first God was "my strength"—representing power to the Israelites. But they did not realize until this moment that God was more than power; that there was lyricism, song, to the world in which God is real. God is more than strength, God is song. And those two features, strength and song, taken together, are salvation.

There is one other poignant feature of this story. Earlier we discussed Moses' inability to speak. Here we find the people at the outset of their wanderings, before they have received the *devarim*, the revelation from God. Yet the song begins: "Moses and the children of Israel sang this song." Even though Moses could not yet truly speak, he could sing.

Song and Celebration

Part of the magic of words is that they can do more than communicate. They can exhilarate. The commemoration of the Exodus event, the holiday of Passover, is an elaborate ritual meal. The meal is filled with charm and ceremony, and central to it is song. From the outset, the melodies are woven into the observance, recalling the joy of liberation and the need to express that joy. At the end of the meal, several songs are strung together like final triumphal steps from the sea. They are puzzle songs designed to entertain children, songs that build step by step,

songs to stir the fancy. They have the light giddiness that
reminds us in some slight way of the ecstasy of finding
oneself free. Liberation has been surrounded by song from
the moment of its inception to its commemoration some
3,500 years later.

Just as liberation from bondage was an occasion for
song, subsequent service to God in Judaism was through
song. Even in the Temple of old, when sacrifices were the
principal mode of worship, the talmudic Rabbi Meir ad-
vises that "song is a necessary complement to sacrifice."
In ancient times the Psalms were sung. The priests in the
Temple performed their ritual obligations to the accompaniment of music. The servants of God were choruses.

Today, if one wishes to see this aspect of the Jewish
tradition, it is on display not only in prayer services, but
at the Sabbath meal. The meals on Sabbath are filled with
zemirot, special songs that mark the spirit of the day. Some
of the songs are fanciful, greeting Sabbath angels, depict-
ing the Sabbath as a bride. Some glorify God. Others take
snatches of verses or well-known sayings and set them to
music. Whatever the particular lyric, the motivation remains the same: once again, joy cannot be bounded by
speech, but must spill over into song.

The most comprehensive example of this in Judaism is
the small midrash called *Perek Shirah*—the chapter of song.
Through its several parts, it depicts the entire world singing out to God, beginning with the heavens and the earth,
moving on to all types of animals, mammals and birds and
fish, then on to plant life, and to all things, animate and
inanimate. Throughout the midrash the song of each part
of creation is fleshed out with verses from the Bible exploring and explaining the ways in which that portion of
the world sings out to God. The overall effect is a uni-

versal chorus singing praises to the Creator. It is a totality
of joy, of music, beyond the imagination of the most daring composer. It is the sound of everything that is pouring
forth its essence in song to God. In the words of the Hebrew writer Micah Joseph Berdechevski: "It is not you
alone, or we, or those others who pray; all things pray,
all things pour forth their souls. The heavens pray, the
earth prays, every creature and every living thing prays.
In all life, there is longing. Creation itself is but a longing,
a kind of prayer to the Almighty."

Learning to study in the Jewish tradition is learning to
sing. The study of Talmud, the back-and-forth of legal
argumentation, was always done in a melody, as a chant.
When talmudic study takes place, one can hear the peculiar lilt, the repetitive rhythms of argument and solution
that were not, classically, expressed in the monotone of
conversation, but in the animated, rolling sound of Jewish
schooling. A student slow to pick up the nuances of the
argument is told that he or she doesn't have the melody.
Study has to soar. As Martin Buber once put it, "The
beating heart of the universe is holy joy." And holy joy
comes out in song.

The same is true of the Bible. The weekly portion that
is read from the Torah in synagogue is not actually read—
it is chanted. Following the Torah portion, a selection
from the prophetic or historical books is also chanted, this
time in a minor key. The haunting strains of the prophets
are not flattened by robbing them of intonation. They are
brought to life with melody.

In the sweetness of the voice of learning, tradition lives.
The material is fixed on the page, it must be learned. Ide-
ally, though, one can hear in the notes of a student's voice
that the learning is not fixed, it is not mere rote recitation,

but is from the heart. The melody invigorates the learning, until the student is truly following the prescription of the prophet: "Sing to the Lord a new song" (Isa. 42:10). The same words become new because they have been elevated from statement to song.

The music of one student studying, just as the music of one person praying, can aid another to reach beyond the self. As Rabbi Pinchas of Koritz said: "When one is singing and cannot lift his voice, and another comes and sings as well, another who can lift his voice, then the first will be able to lift his voice as well. That is the secret of the bond between spirit and spirit."

Celebration is a subject of song, and so is love. The only book in the Bible designated a song is the Song of Songs. Traditionally ascribed to King Solomon, the son of David, it reinforces the notion of a monarch who could sing. The Song is of love: "Oh, give me the kisses of your mouth, For your love is more delightful than wine. . . . Set me as a seal upon your heart, For love is as strong as death; vast floods cannot quench it, nor rivers drown it" (Song of Songs 1:2, 8:6,7). The Rabbis understood this poem to be an allegory for the love between God and Israel. The song expresses attachment, love, and joy. So expressive and important is this love song that Rabbi Akiva said: "All of scripture is holy, but *The Song of Songs* is the Holy of Holies."

Powerful as the image of joyous song can be, however, song is necessary in solemn moments as well. "Just as atonement for sin is indispensable," teaches the Midrash, "so too is song indispensable." Just as we must beseech forgiveness, we must express ourselves in song. Yom Kippur, the day of atonement, is the most solemn time in the Jewish year. Throughout the day there is song. Voices are lifted in praise, in confession and admonition. The Kol Nidre chant is the most resonant melody of the entire Jewish year.

Even calamity is commemorated with elegies. The book of Lamentations etches in memorable strokes the pain of exile from the land of Israel. Jerusalem, the beloved city, is desolate. The people are bereft and hopeless: "How the city sits solitary, that was full of people. She that was great among nations, princess among the provinces—She has become a captive" (Lam. 1:1). Each year during Tisha B'av, the day that commemorates the destruction of the Temple, the book of Lamentations is sung. The melancholy tune reminds the listener how tortured were the spirits of those who saw the end of their country, of their civilization, who beheld the ruins of their Temple. Yet at the same time, because the book of Lamentations is sung, it hints at another song, a song of the future, a song of redemption.

The Song of Redemption

When the great Hebrew poet Yehuda Halevy sings to Zion, imagining a day when the scattered will be returned, he proclaims: "When I dream of your return from captivity, I am a harp for all your songs." Redemption is the occasion for song. The land, and the heavens, are listening.

A Chasidic interpretation of the phrase "Song of Songs" is that the repetition of the word "song" implies that the songs sung down here, on earth, affect the songs sung above, in heaven.

There has always been a connection in the Jewish psyche between redemption and song. Part of the bond is that song is often an expression of joy, of the rightness of things. Part of it is that song was so intimately intertwined with worship at the Temple in Jerusalem, a symbol of redemption. And part of it is also that the ability to feel joy, to give it expression, is a demonstration that one is ready for and even worthy of being redeemed.

In the Talmud we find an unusual deliberation. God is pondering the possibility of making King Hezekiah the Messiah. He was a righteous king and possessed many of the qualities necessary for one who would deliver his people and the world from its travail and trouble. But in the end, in this talmudic legend, God decides that Hezekiah cannot be the Messiah. Why? Because throughout the king's life God has performed various miracles for him. God has, as we noted before, heard King Hezekiah's prayer and seen his tears. Yet despite all the wonders and favors God has showered upon him, King Hezekiah, unlike King David, did not sing before God. And song is a necessary accompaniment to redemption. One cannot be the Messiah if one's soul is fettered, if the heart is locked up—if one's spirit has no song.

In his poem "Sailing to Byzantium," Yeats beautifully expresses the idea that learning, that studying, is how the soul can sing. He wrote: "Nor is there singing school but studying. . . . O sages standing in God's holy fire . . . be the singing-masters of my soul." The sages—in the case of the Jewish tradition, the Rabbis—are the singing masters of the soul. They mark out the trail that, if followed, enables a soul to soar. They guide us along the path of praise, the ways of study; they teach us how to sing. Without song, faith is a dry, desiccated shell. Joy is part of the spark that kindles conviction and brings faith to life.

The imagery of song is pervasive in Judaism, touching all aspects of the tradition. When the Psalmist wishes to praise something, he calls it a song. Thus, in speaking of the joy of observing God's law, the Psalmist writes: "Your laws are songs for me wherever I may dwell" (Ps. 119:54). The comparison helps us to understand just how beloved and how joyous God's law is to the Psalmist—so cherished that it has the status of song.

With song we have moved to what is in some ways the fullest possible expression of the soul. Words in song and poetry are compact, sonorous, bursting. With song we have reached toward the essence of the word.

Still, it seems there is more to say. Perhaps that is why songs that vault past the confines of words are so prominent in the Jewish tradition. *Niggunim*, songs without words, songs that are pure melody, constitute some of the highest expressions of praise, some of the most exalted flights of religious transport. For the yearning spirit is always seeking to say more, to follow the biblical admonition "Pour out your heart like water in the presence of the Lord" (Lam. 2:19). At times, saying more, truly pouring out one's heart, is to abandon words altogether. At times melodies can soar past the realm of definitions and explanations.

When we have reached the outer boundaries of utterance, when we have sung so that the notes have sounded our souls as far as they are able, when the totality of language seems exhausted and there is yet more inside of us, we are in need of something that transcends the word. We search for that plane that is above even song, that cannot be articulated or intoned.

Words carry us to the farthest reaches of understanding, and then they fail. Melody can liberate emotion, but something escapes; there remains a purpose and a passion that transcend it. If we can continue to follow the arc of meaning inside us, song will lead us to silence.

NINE

~

The Cry of
Silence

The altar dearest to God is the altar of silence.

CHASIDIC SAYING

We began with a personal struggle against silence. This book was sparked by the experience of watching someone I love battle with wordlessness.

The image of that struggle stood behind all these explorations, behind the discussion of the power and salience of words in our lives. What is it to speak, and to be unable to speak? What is lost—and is anything gained? My mother has recovered a halting use of speech. At times she can find the word she is seeking. Often, it eludes her. Sometimes when my mother pronounces a word or phrase there is a sense, not of joy (as there was at first), but of fleeting satisfaction that things are working properly, this time. No longer is each new word a possible harbinger of total recovery. It is just a frustration averted. When the words will not come, there is defeat, and a mute longing.

That longing always produces a strained silence. It is a silence that is forced, not chosen, and its qualities are different from those of other silences. Experience with silence teaches how soundlessness wears many guises. It is silence that outlines and overbounds the world, as it does our own lives. We emerge from silence, and return to it. In our daily lives, at certain moments, the tumble of words ceases, and we find that lurking outside each sentence is a silence. Often we ignore it or fend it off, for the silence makes us uneasy. Yet we know that when we have passed through words, there is a stillness waiting. If we are strong enough at times we can exist in that silence, and find meaning in it, as does the Psalmist: "Truly my soul waits silently for God" (Ps. 62:2).

In these pages we have been scouting and surveying the domain of words, watching them as they encouraged, revealed, misled, betrayed, taught, nurtured our souls. All the while it was manifest that we would have to end where we began. After all the talking, once again, what remains to us is silence.

The qualities of that silence will vary. There are silences of bewilderment and loss, of indignation and anger. There are silences of service, of celebration. There are silences of expectation, and of endings. There are silences that explain, and silences that reject all explanation. One mystical tradition teaches that all God revealed at Sinai was the letter aleph—the first letter of the Hebrew alphabet, which is a silent letter. All explanation is contained in the silence. The totality of God's revelation to humanity is in a single letter that bears no sound; the richness of such a silence defies imagination. The silence encompasses all words, and transcends them.

The philosopher Wittgenstein said, "The limits of my language are the limits of my world." To go beyond the limits of one's world, nothing will serve but silence.

The Outcry of Silence

A friend and former teacher, Rabbi Gordon Tucker, told me the following story. For several weeks after the birth of his first child, the newborn baby would cry in the middle of the night. Each night Ethan cried, regularly, predictably. Each night his father and mother would run to the cradle, watching him, comforting him. Bleary-eyed but happy, his parents knew they could count on their newborn's midnight screams. Then one night, Ethan did not cry. There was no sound. His father woke up in the middle of the night, startled and frightened. The silence terrified him. He ran to the crib, certain something was wrong. There he saw his son sleeping peacefully, healthy and safe. That silence, said Gordon, that silence of Ethan's not crying, was louder than any scream.

At times, the silence cuts deeper than any words. It can pound and howl. The silent cry pierces the heavens. Edvard Munch's famous painting *The Scream* is all the more powerful because the observer *sees* the scream, but cannot hear it. One sees the tortured face and opened mouth of a man screaming on a bridge, his hands cradling his face. But the agony of the picture is in its absence—the absence of any sound. It is the cry that we keep anticipating, but that never comes. It exists only in the imagination of the onlooker. And the silent scream that we recreate in our own minds overwhelms us.

The power of silence is represented in the Bible by the short, painful story of Aaron's sons, Nadab and Abihu:

> Now Aaron's sons Nadab and Abihu each took his
> fire pan, put fire in it, and laid incense on it; and
> they offered alien fire before the Lord, which He
> had not enjoined upon them. And fire came forth
> from the Lord and consumed them. . . . And Aaron
> was silent. (Lev. 10:1–3)

For reasons that are not clear in the passage, the lives of
two of Aaron's sons, Nadab and Abihu, have come to a
terrible, sudden end. Their father is shocked and grieved.
And he is silent.

What is the nature of Aaron's silence? The Bible gives
us no sense of what Aaron is feeling, or the deeper meaning of his silence. Is it the silence of absolute agony, so
profound it cannot find words? Is it the silence of self-
blame, of rage, of frustration, of terror for himself and his
remaining sons?

Perhaps what Aaron is really expressing is still more
challenging. Perhaps in his silence there is a reproach—a
reproach to God for God's own silence. Where are Your
words, Aaron may be asking. Where are Your words of
warning, or even after the fact, words of explanation? Or
could it even be that Aaron's sons acted in disregard of
their own father's instructions, and his silence is the silence of acceptance, of resignation?

Whatever the meaning, a lesson of Aaron's silence is
that for certain moments, times of tremendous emotion or
meaning, only silence will suffice. Words, no matter how
apt or eloquent, would limit, confine, circumscribe the experience. Could there be any words adequate to describe
what Aaron must have endured at that moment? Surely
an attempt to frame his emotions in language runs the risk
of debasing the experience. On the other hand, the po-

tency of his silence is unmistakable. In saying nothing, Aaron has said far more than could be spoken. Ecclesiastes reminds us that there is "a time for silence and a time for speaking" (3:7). The Rabbis, commenting on that verse, ask, "When is a time for silence? In the moments of mourning." When loss cuts too deep there are no words. So Aaron was silent.

Rabbi Menachem Mendle of Kotzk said, "The cry one holds back is the most powerful of all."

No silence is more powerful, more potent, than God's. In a world that cries out at times for a guiding word, the heavens are mute. Speaking of idols, the Psalmist writes that "they have mouths, but cannot speak" (Ps. 115:5). How much more wrenching to think of a God who could speak, who can speak, who will not speak.

This has been the indictment of God throughout the ages. Why, the faithful ask, are You silent? Why, ask those who are tried beyond endurance, will You not speak in times of calamity? "O God, do not be silent. Do not stay aloof. Do not be still!" (Ps. 83:2).

God acknowledges the silence. "I have kept silent from of old, kept still and restrained Myself" (Isa. 42:14). God then promises to remedy the silence, to cry out, to overturn the order of the world, to make darkness light and rough places into level ground. Through Isaiah, God assures us that the end of silence is at hand. It is a prophecy and pledge yet to be realized.

The drama of religious history has been to hear the strain of a voice through the silence. Perhaps the core of faith can be defined as the certainty that even in the silence there is a message. It is the paradox of listening for that which cannot be heard. The realization that part of the music resides in the spaces between the notes.

Isaiah is preoccupied with God's silence and distance. He foresees that one day God will be manifest, and the nations of the world will proclaim, "You are indeed a God who concealed Himself" (Isa. 45:15). Surely they would be right to feel that God has been hiding. But the real burden of the lesson is not that God was hidden, but that Isaiah felt sure that God would emerge; that he kept searching; that he heard the silence as a promise.

Imagine the children of Israel walking through the desert, with its vast stillness. Day after day they march through the sloping, silent wilderness. Even the slightest sounds are as a thunderclap in the wasteland. During the march, they dream of hearing a voice cut through silence. They dream of a sound to light up the sky.

The metaphor is strange and mixed: how can a sound light up the sky? Can sound be seen?

The first words after the giving of the ten commandments read literally, "And all the people saw the voices" (Exod. 20:15). The ways in which God spoke were somehow visible. Apparently, sound can be seen.

As with any seeming paradox in the Bible, the commentators rush in, each armed with clarification: the phrase really means that one could see the effect of the voice in people's lives as they rushed to obey God's will; or that the voice made the world tremble, so its effect was visible as well as audible; or perhaps that the world was at that moment turned upside down so that what up to now had been seen (images of God in pagan cultures) could only be heard and what had been heard (voices and commands) could actually be seen.

However we understand "saw the voices," it is clearly intended to be the pinnacle of the word. Verbal expression has become so real that it engages all the senses. For once the silence is broken, the desert seems alive, the world pulses and dances.

Such a celebration of communication may touch us, but we still wonder: where is the voice *we* can see, where is the word that drops out of the sky, transforming both the desert and our own souls? More and more it might seem that the silence of Aaron in the face of tragedy is not reproach, or even anger, but mocking—This is how you sound to me, God, Aaron seems to be saying. I stand here, in the midst of tragedy, among the ashes, and you are silent. "I cry out to You," says Job, "but You do not answer me" (Job 30:20).

So Aaron and revelation stand as alternate symbols— one as the totality of the word, the other as the awful side of silence. Aaron's is the silence of frustration, of not hearing the voice, of not answering, not being able to speak. The silence of Aaron, the mirror of God's, is one that wrenches the soul, and his refusal to cry out is a terrible accusation of the unfairness of it all. In this web of words, Aaron seems to be saying, I will cut past them, I will indict in silence.

The Silence of Service

Judaism tends to associate service with deeds and with words. Yet we can also serve with stillness, serve with silence.

The great scholar Rabbi Elijah of Wilna once advised his students that it is often more effective to fast with words than with food. A fast of words, a struggle with silence, can teach us how often we misuse them. To be without words refurbishes our sense of their radiance. Silence can create space above the chatter. It allows one to hear that which might be otherwise ignored.

Silence in the Bible is a school for prophecy. It helps train the prophet to listen. Words, heard and unheard, spoken and held back, are central to the prophetic mission. Since a prophet must understand the place of words, so a prophet must appreciate silence.

In the third chapter of Ezekiel (verses 1–3), God teaches the prophet the value of words in a dramatic way. "God said to me,—'Mortal, eat what is offered to you; eat this scroll, and go speak to the House of Israel.' So I opened my mouth, and He gave me this scroll to eat as He said to me, 'Mortal, feed your stomach and fill your belly with this scroll that I give you.' I ate it, and it tasted as sweet as honey to me." Ezekiel's prophecy is inaugurated by the actual physical consumption of a scroll—ingesting the words.

At the end of the same chapter, however, God says to Ezekiel: "I will make your tongue cleave to your palate, and you shall be dumb" (3:26). Having tasted the power of words, Ezekiel will also be trained in silence. Thirty chapters later, we read: "Now the hand of the Lord had come upon me the evening before . . . and He opened my mouth . . . thus my mouth was opened and I was no longer speechless" (33:22). Once schooled in silence, the prophet can speak.

Silence can be a powerful teacher. In Chaim Potok's charged novel *The Chosen*, he portrays how in certain homes silence was used as an educative tool—a tool less of distance than of love. It was a silence that, even when austere, was filled with a tenderness, a warmth that could not quite reach words. Some silence can draw close, even while retaining the mystery and the distance that creeps between any two people struggling to understand each other. Rabbi Simeon, the son of Gamliel, said: "All my life I was brought up among the sages, and I have found nothing better for a person than silence."

We feel the sense of embracing silence in Psalm 19. Earlier we quoted the Psalm in one of two possible translations. The Psalm begins: "The heavens declare the glory of God, the sky proclaims His handiwork. Each day declares, each night expresses knowledge." The next line in Hebrew reads: *"Ayn omer . . . b'li nishma kolam."* This can be interpreted to mean "there is no speech whose sound goes unheard" or "there are no words—their voice is not heard." In one case it teaches the value of words, in the other how cherished is silence. The same phrase serves both sides of the message. But in either case the opening affirmation "The heavens declare the glory of God" remains. Whether that declaration is couched in the glitter of words or in the black sheen of silence, it points back to God.

In silence as in speech there may be service.

Silence as Celebration

"To You," sings the Psalmist to God, "silence is praise" (Ps. 65:2). When we are struck dumb by the wonder of the world, we are praising God. When we are touched so deeply that words will not emerge, we are led back to the Source of meaning.

Even the silence of nature can be praise of God. The book of Joshua speaks of Joshua's asking God for a miracle, and relates that in response, the sun stood still. Actually the Hebrew word used is *dom*, which can also be translated as "silent." The sun stood silent for Joshua, and in that silence was acknowledgment of God's presence and sovereignty.

Silence can be a way of permitting space to remain within ourselves, a way of seeking to let God in. We do not crowd out presence with a jumble of internal words. We seek a stillness. We rest in silence, and through it pray.

The practice of *hitbodedut*, the temporary separation of the self from the hum and bustle of daily life in order to meditate upon God, is a long-established practice in Judaism. *Hitbodedut*—literally, "aloneness"—is a technique of temporary isolation. The soul, seeking solitude, seeking quiet, searches out a place where the sounds of the world recede. Once that place is found, the spirit can stand single before its Creator. *Hitbodedut* helps the soul hear its own voice. At first that voice may be wild, shrill. But in time the soul quiets, the silence is permitted to speak, and the aloneness ceases to be aloneness—it becomes togetherness with the Creator. Free from distraction, the soul finds through the surrounding silence an avenue back to God.

There are moments in our lives, not of jubilation but of serene, supreme joy, when we understand the deep bliss that can be spoken only through silence. There are moments when we tap into the current of goodness, of *shlemut*, of completion, that courses through the world, and are silently reminded that the celebration of silence is deep indeed. A word, any word, wrote Wittgenstein, strikes a note on the keyboard of imagination. Surely this is so. Each word strikes a note. But a word, like a note, is limited, confined to its own place on the musical register. Silence can contain within it all the music that can be played, for all of it emerges from silence. A word is a note. Silence is a symphony.

Beyond Words

Ultimately, there are places beyond words. Perhaps we can only get there by traversing the wilderness, by making our way through words, to the other side. At times, the only path is to first exhaust other kinds of communication: words and tears and song. But in the end there are messages in silence that cannot be spoken.

In the Bible, throughout the story of the flood, Noah is silent. He follows God's command, builds the ark, assembles the animals, but he does not speak. No words could possibly be adequate—what can one say in the face of certain destruction? We are invited to imagine the turmoil inside of Noah. We are not confined or kept out by his words.

The same is true with Abraham, when God asks him to sacrifice his son Isaac (Gen., chapter 22). Throughout that brief but harrowing episode, Abraham responds through action. Abraham keeps his own counsel. We are invited to imagine the storm that rages inside him. Indeed, generations of midrashists and commentators have sought to fill in the gaps left them by Abraham's reticence. The literature is rich with stories about what happened in Abraham's soul, things that he thought and said which were not recorded. Yet the Bible remains more riveting than any tale which seeks to supplement it. "There is no voice, there are no words." There is nothing to say. Abraham's silence is infinitely more powerful than any word.

In the Bible, the prophet Elijah stands upon the mountain to encounter the Presence of God. "And lo, the Lord passed by. There was a great and mighty wind, splitting mountains and shattering rocks by the power of the Lord; but the Lord was not in the wind. After the wind—an earthquake; but the Lord was not in the earthquake. After the earthquake—fire, but the Lord was not in the fire. And after the fire, a still, small voice" (1 Kings 19:11, 12).

The theologian Andre Neher has pointed out that the literal translation of "a still small voice" is "a thin voice of silence." Elijah was witness to a titanic show of natural force in order to prepare him to listen for the silence. He was anticipating a word, and needed to learn to hear its absence. God's self-disclosure to Elijah is not with a word, but with the voice of silence. Elijah is renowned for his zeal; he understands the God of awesome declarations, of dazzling wonders. In the previous chapter, Elijah, in opposition to the priests of the idol Baal, has invoked God's fire upon an altar. Now when God needs to speak to him, Elijah expects thunder. He learns silence.

Perhaps when we feel the lack of God's voice most keenly, perhaps when God is most silent, inside ourselves it is the opportunity to listen to the voice we cannot hear.

Listening to that which cannot be heard seems too much a paradox until one recalls the words of Rabbi Menachem Mendel of Vorki. Asked what characterizes an ideal Jew, he replied, "Upright kneeling, silent screaming, motionless dance." One who can be broken, and thus whole. One who can listen to the silence, for the silence can speak.

Children from the Chamber of Yearnings

This book is a meditation on words that was launched by my mother's and my family's personal tragedy. I wanted to find out, by rummaging through the meaning of words as an individual and as a Jew, what my mother had lost. What were these pervasive things, in our throats, in our hearts, stuck to our souls, these sounds that surround each moment of life, that grant us intimacy and knowledge, inspiration, warning, laughter? I wanted to begin to understand what we do when we speak to one another, and when we speak to God; not what we do scientifically, or even anthropologically, but what we do spiritually. The task was to understand something about how our faith shapes our communication, and how our communication shapes our faith. The Jewish tradition, with its reverence for words and its strains of silence, was ideal ground for such exploration. Perhaps it could help decipher the inner language of faith, and even help us to reclaim it.

For I knew that although my mother's speech has returned to some extent, her loss is enormous and irrevocable. Seeking to understand that loss meant an exploration of our reliance on the word.

Yet I also knew that even in the moments when she was almost completely robbed of words, she was not robbed of expression. My mother is gifted with an eloquent face, but it was not only her "facial phrases," her looks and glances; it was what she could say in her silence, which could, and can, carry beyond words.

For what was lost was specific information. Silence cannot offer particular, exact messages. It cannot proffer details; to tell someone a name, a place, to describe an incident, one needs words. But to convey love, sorrow, pride, a look is often more compelling, a quiet gleam more powerful than any word. In the silence, in the messages that transcend words, in the language of the eyes, there is eloquence. As Posthumus says to his absent Imogen in Shakespeare's *Cymbeline*, "I'll speak to thee in silence."

To carry beyond words, to achieve expression of that which cannot be said, is inestimably precious. This most emphatically my mother retains. Her silences are eloquent, brimming with meaning, explosive, expansive, understanding, understood. The central messages of life remain.

The *Zohar*, the great text of Jewish mysticism, speaks of those with acute spiritual hunger as being "children from the chamber of yearnings." We are all children from that chamber, feeling inside in our best moments that our yearnings cannot find full expression, that our exhilaration, and our pain, remain somehow buried so deep that no articulation can unearth them, can bring them to light. "In each word," teaches the *Zohar*, "shines many lights." But sometimes we need to express the darkness. Longings cannot always be held up to light.

We understand, we children of the chamber, that our deepest cries are silent.

The guiding image of the Bible is that of God transmitting truth through words. But that is only a stage on our journey. One day perhaps we will be able to reach beyond words, to break through the frustration of inarticulateness, to cease searching for how to say what remains inside us. One day we will be able to express eternity in a glance.

The assurance of that time is found in the prophet Zephaniah. Like so many masters of the word, Zephaniah knows that we must transcend it. And in speaking to the people he envisions a time of peace, a time when "You need fear tragedy no more." On that day all will be as it should be. On that day, says the prophet, "God will be silent in love" (Zeph. 3:17).

In its way, Zephaniah's is the most comprehensive prophecy ever spoken. For it foresees a world in which human relationships, in which prophecy itself, will no longer be shackled and shaped by what we can say.

Even in the absence of utterance we will be certain of connection.

"God will be silent in love." God works through words, and reaches toward silence. And we, all of us, are fashioned in the image of God.

Know that it is possible

to let out a very great scream

in a voice that no one will hear.

No sound actually emerges—

the scream takes place within the silence.

Everyone is capable of such a cry.

RABBI NACHMAN OF BRATZLAV

Index

Index of Biblical Citations